J 550 Van
Van Rose, Susanna
Earth /

34028081820400
FB $19.99 ocn851509724
07/16/13

D0919486

EYEWITNESS BOOKS
MONEY
MOON
MUMMY
MUSIC

MYTHOLOGY
NASCAR
NATURAL DISASTERS
NORTH AMERICAN INDIAN
OCEAN
OIL
OLYMPICS
PERSPECTIVE
PHOTOGRAPHY
PIRATE
PLANT
POND & RIVER
PREDATOR
PREHISTORIC LIFE
PRESIDENTS
PYRAMID
RELIGION
RENAISSANCE
REPTILE
RESCUE
ROBOT
ROCKS & MINERALS
RUSSIA
SCIENCE
SEASHORE
SHAKESPEARE
SHARK
SHELL
SHIPWRECK
SKELETON
SOCCER
SOLDIER
SPACE EXPLORATION
SPORTS
SPY
SUBMARINE
SUPER BOWL
TECHNOLOGY
TEXAS
TIME & SPACE
TITANIC
TRAIN
TRANSPORTATION
TREASURE
TREE
UNIVERSE
VAN GOGH
VIETNAM WAR
VIKING
VOLCANO & EARTHQUAKE
VOTE
WATER
WATERCOLOR
WEATHER
WHALE
WILD WEST
WITCHES & MAGIC-MAKERS
WORLD SERIES
WORLD WAR I
WORLD WAR II

WITHDRAWN

Eyewitness
EARTH

William Smith (1769–1839)

Monoclinic crystals of sulfur

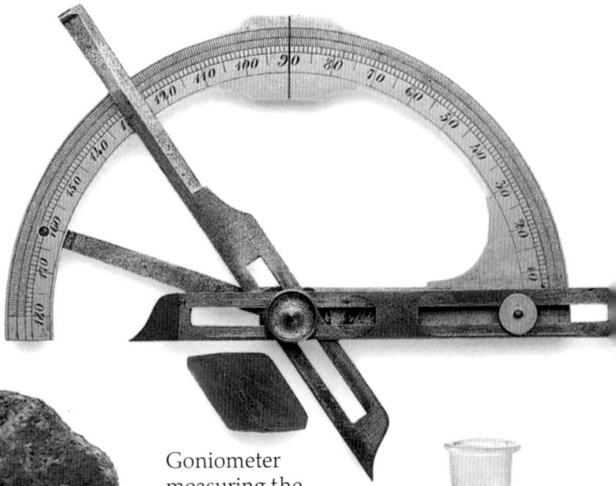

Goniometer measuring the angles on a copper sulfate crystal

Eclogite rock

Granite rock

Metallic copper

An orrery showing the Earth's orbit around the Sun

Malachite in a rock

Laboratory model imitating a mountain range

Eyewitness
EARTH

Written by
SUSANNA VAN ROSE

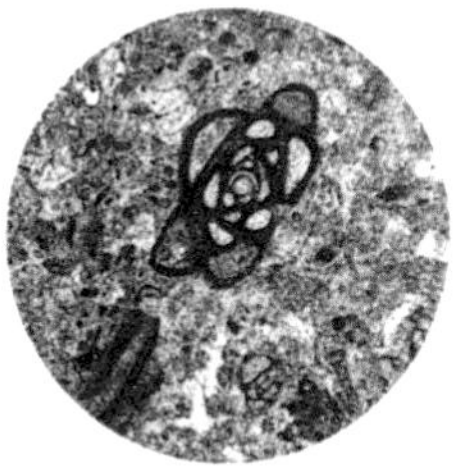
Magnified thin section of limestone

Garden snails provided a clue to the continental drift theory

Gondwanaland

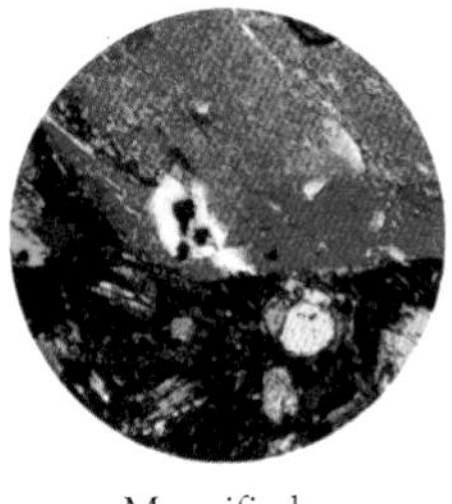
Magnified thin section of gabbro rock

Adding carbon dioxide to water

Natural gold crystals in a piece of quartz rock

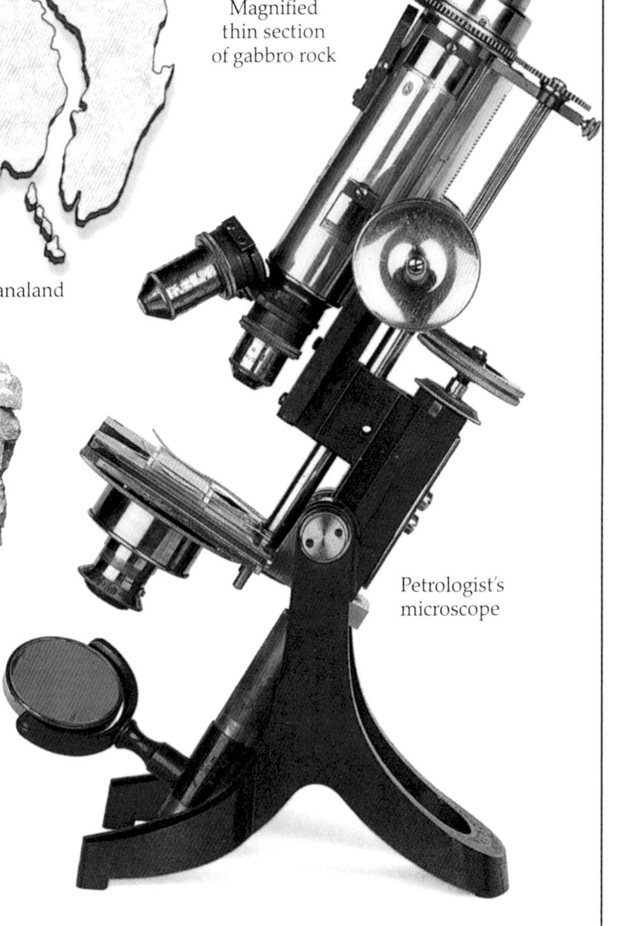
Petrologist's microscope

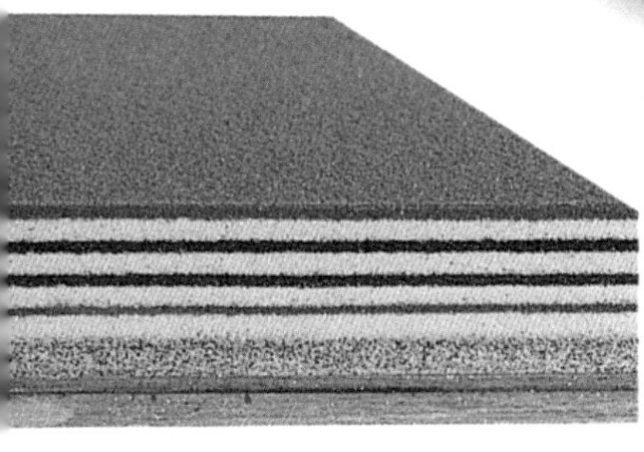

Sifting fossils
from seafloor
sediments

Rapid cooling
of heated sulfur

**LONDON, NEW YORK,
MELBOURNE, MUNICH, and DELHI**

Project Editor Charyn Jones
Art Editor Jane Bull
Design Assistant Helen Diplock
Production Adrian Gathercole
Special photography Clive Streeter
Picture Research Caroline Brooke
Managing Editor Josephine Buchanan
Managing Art Editor Lynne Brown
Editorial Consultant Dr. John Cope,
University of Wales College of Cardiff, Wales
US Editor Charles A. Wills
US Consultant Professor Warren Yasso
Teachers College, Columbia University

Revised Edition
Revised by John Woodward

DK INDIA
Project editor Shatarupa Chaudhuri
Project art editor Nishesh Batnagar
Assistant editor Priyanka Kharbanda
Assistant art editor Honlung Zach Ragui
DTP designer Tarun Sharma
Picture researcher Sumedha Chopra

DK UK
Senior editor Caroline Stamps
Senior art editor Rachael Grady
Pre-production producers Adam Stoneham
and Rachel Ng
Publisher Andrew Macintyre

DK US
US editor Margaret Parrish
Editorial director Nancy Ellwood

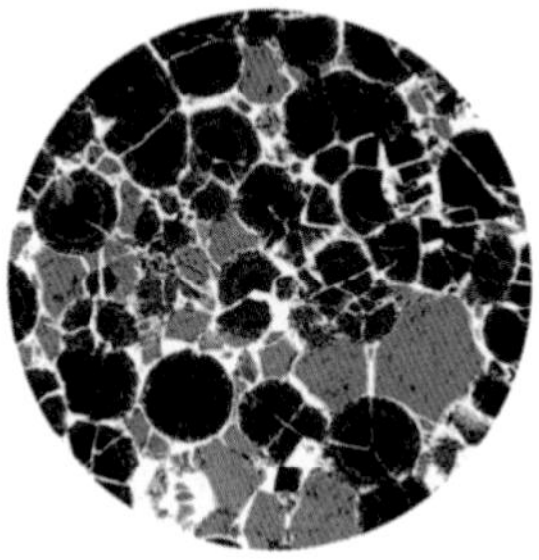

Microscopic thin
section of obsidian

Heating powdered sulfur

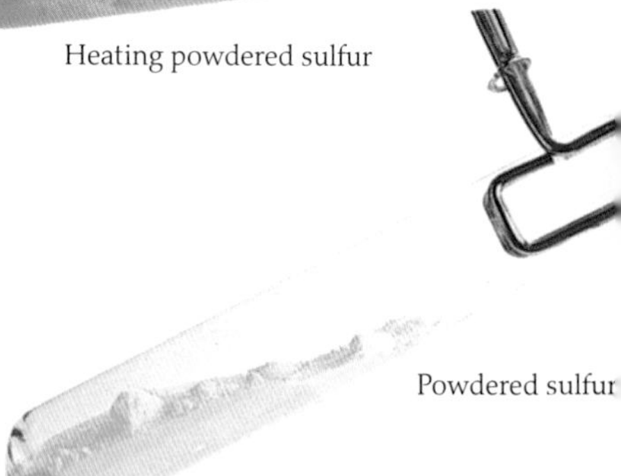

Powdered sulfur

This revised edition published in the United States in 2013
by DK Publishing, 345 Hudson Street
New York, New York 10014
First published in the United States in 1994

13 14 15 16 17 10 9 8 7 6 5 4 3 2 1

001–187806–June/13

Copyright © 1994, © 2005, © 2013 Dorling Kindersley Limited
All rights reserved under International and Pan-American Copyright Conventions. No part of this publication may be reproduced, stored in a retrieval system, or transmitted in any form or by any means, electronic, mechanical, photocopying, recording, or otherwise, without the prior written permission of the copyright owner. Published in Great Britain by Dorling Kindersley Limited.

DK books are available at special discounts when purchased in bulk for sales promotions, premiums, fundraising, or educational use. For details, contact: DK Publishing Special Markets, 345 Hudson Street, New York, New York 10014
SpecialSales@dk.com

A catalog record for this book is available from the Library of Congress.

ISBN: 978-1-4654-0897-6
ISBN: 978-1-4654-0898-3 (Library binding)

Color reproduction by Alta Image
Printed in China by South China Printing Company

A goniometer for
measuring the
angles of crystals

Discover more at
www.dk.com

James Hutton (1726–1797)

Contents

Samples collected by the *Challenger* (1872–1876)

What makes up the Earth?

As a small planet in the vast solar system, the Earth is unique in a number of ways. It has life, it has water, and it has a surface (thin rocky crust) that is continually being renewed, especially on the deep ocean floors. The parts of the Earth that can be seen are just a tiny proportion of the whole planet. Beneath the crust lies the thick, many-layered mantle, which is also rocky, and at the center there is a metal core, which is partly solid and partly liquid. The planet is surrounded by a magnetic field, which fluctuates with time and blots out the intense radiations from the Sun that would be harmful to life. The rocky silicate crust is enveloped in a shroud of water and atmospheric gases (pp. 10–11) that have almost entirely come from the eruptions of volcanoes over time. The crust is made up of segments known as plates that move around slowly; over millions of years this movement changes the architecture of the continents as the plates interact (pp. 36–37).

SATELLITE VIEW OF EARTH
The Earth is not exactly spherica in shape. It is flattened at the pole with a bulge at the equator so that t radius at the poles is 27 miles (43 k shorter than the equatorial radius. T ancient Greek philosopher Pythago (c. 570–500 BCE) thought that th Earth might be spherical in shape. T idea came to him as he watched shi approach from over the horizon. Fi he saw their masts; only as they car closer did the hulls appear.

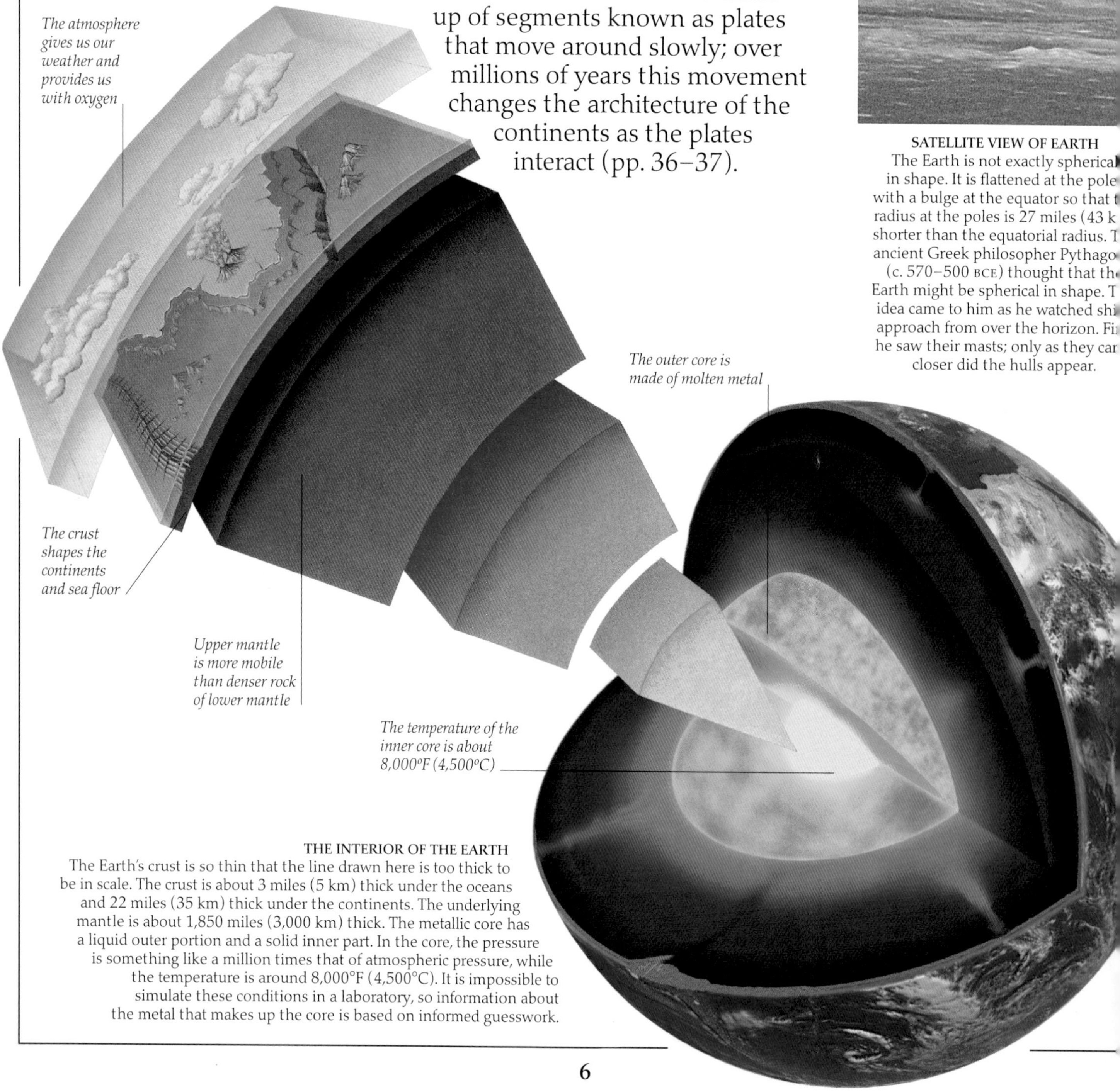
The atmosphere gives us our weather and provides us with oxygen
The outer core is made of molten metal
The crust shapes the continents and sea floor
Upper mantle is more mobile than denser rock of lower mantle
The temperature of the inner core is about 8,000°F (4,500°C)

THE INTERIOR OF THE EARTH
The Earth's crust is so thin that the line drawn here is too thick to be in scale. The crust is about 3 miles (5 km) thick under the oceans and 22 miles (35 km) thick under the continents. The underlying mantle is about 1,850 miles (3,000 km) thick. The metallic core has a liquid outer portion and a solid inner part. In the core, the pressure is something like a million times that of atmospheric pressure, while the temperature is around 8,000°F (4,500°C). It is impossible to simulate these conditions in a laboratory, so information about the metal that makes up the core is based on informed guesswork.

he Earth's ingredients

ide from water, air, and rocks, ding out what the rest of the Earth nade up of is not always possible). 40–41). Some upper mantle :ks are seen at the surface in volcanic iptions of magma (p. 25). These give es to the composition of the mantle. s even more difficult to imagine the nditions of the highly compressed etal at the Earth's solid core. This is e densest part of the Earth because s under great pressure.

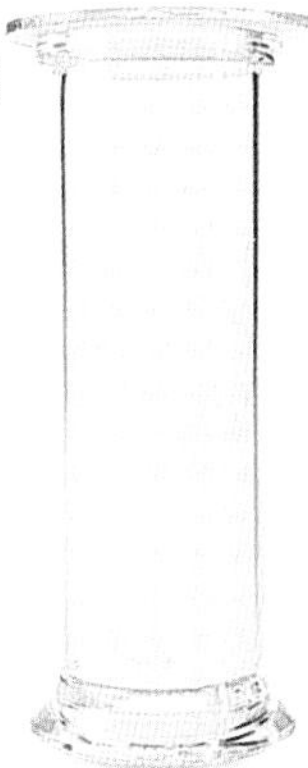

Gas

ATMOSPHERIC GAS
A very small part of 1 percent of the total mass of the Earth.
• The atmosphere is densest close to the surface of the Earth and becomes progressively less dense farther out. Most of the gas molecules are kept to the surface by the Earth's gravity.

Ice

ICE IN GLACIERS AND SHEETS
• About 0.002 percent of the total volume of the Earth.
• 0.003 percent of the total mass of the Earth.
• The ice sheets of the present day are an inheritance from the Ice Age of the last two million years.

Oceanic crust (basalt)

Continental crust (granite)

THE CRUST
• 0.8 percent of the total volume of the Earth.
• 0.4 percent of the total mass of the Earth.
• Oceanic crust is mostly basalt rock made of silicate rich in iron and magnesium.
• Continental rock is a mixture of granitelike rocks, metamorphic rocks, and sedimentary rocks.

Water

WATER
• About 0.1 percent of the total volume of the Earth.
• 0.02 percent of the total mass of the Earth.
• Water is a unique substance that covers three-quarters of the Earth's surface (pp. 16–17).

TAL CORE
6 percent of the total volume he Earth.
1 percent of the total ss of the Earth.

RLY COLLECTORS
dying different rocks gives information out the many processes involved in e changing surface of the Earth. Mary nning (1799–1847) was a fossil collector ng in the west of England. She found sils in ancient rock layers that had en exposed at the surface. Her friend e English geologist Sir Henry De Beche (1796–1855) used this ormation. He established the t national Geological Survey Great Britain in 1835.

THE LIQUID CORE
• Believed to be made of liquid nickel-iron, it is presumed to flow, creating the currents that generate the Earth's magnetic field.

Solid nickel-iron

Solid metal at the core may look like this

Nickel-iron meteorite

THE SOLID CORE
• Some meteorites are made of iron mixed with nickel. It is likely that these are fragments of ancient planet cores, and that Earth's solid core is made of the same metal.

THE MANTLE
• 83 percent of the total volume of the Earth.
• 68 percent of the total mass of the Earth.
• Composed of dense silicate minerals rich in the heavy element, iron; probably it is made of dense, olivine-rich rocks like peridotite. Over the whole history of the Earth, the mantle must slowly have been changing its composition, as magma has been added to the crust, taking away from the upper mantle the chemical elements that melt most easily.

Early ideas about the Earth

MANY EARLY CONCEPTS about the origin and makeup of the Eart were well founded in observation and reason; others were long-held traditions. Sometimes there is a connection between traditional ideas and scientific thought. At other times, it is hard to see any relationship. The development of knowledge and understanding about our surroundings has not always followed a straight line. Although the ancient Greeks and Egyptians established that the Earth was round and calculated its radius with great accuracy, many centuries later some people still believed that the Earth was flat. Early maps were made of local areas and were drawn on flat cloth, so the idea of a flat Earth was a logical extension of the flat-map representation. Early explorers, some of them careful observers, travel extensively and extended knowledge about coastlines and new lands and oceans. In the 18th century one of the earliest modern geologists, James Hutton (1726–97), put forward pioneering idea about the Earth processes. Leaving aside inherited ideas, he worked from observation.

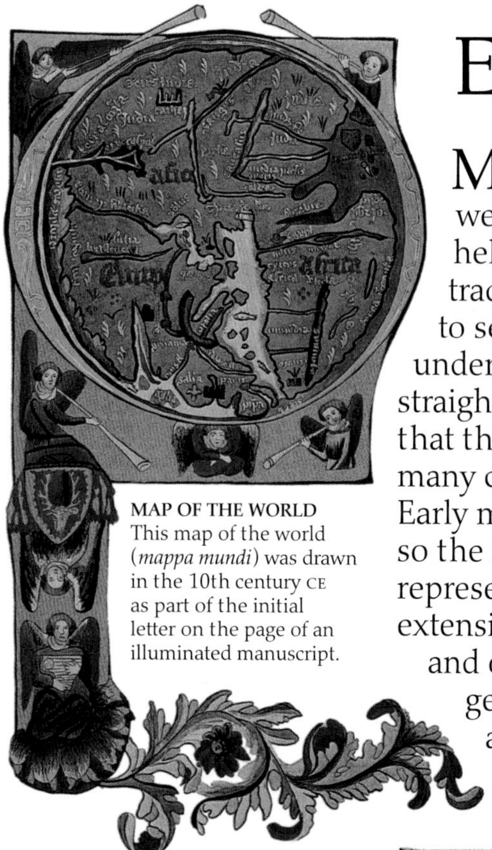

MAP OF THE WORLD
This map of the world (*mappa mundi*) was drawn in the 10th century CE as part of the initial letter on the page of an illuminated manuscript.

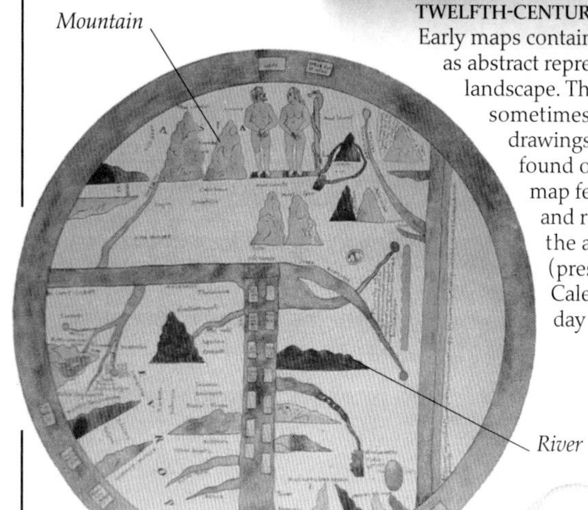

TWELFTH-CENTURY WORLD MAP
Early maps contained pictures as well as abstract representations of the landscape. These pictures were sometimes of the gods, or drawings of the places to be found on the route. This map features mountains and rivers and covers the area from Babylonia (present-day Iraq) to Caledonia (present-day Scotland).

IN SEARCH OF METALS
Divining the landscape, whether for water, for minerals, or for auspicious sites, is followed even today in some technological societies. In his book, *De Re Metallica*, Georg Bauer, a German doctor, philosopher, and mineralogist also known as Georgius Agricola (1494–1555), describes the physical properties of minerals, where metals are found, and how to extract them. He also illustrated the use of forked twigs. He remained sceptical about the usefulness of divination, but admitted that some people were successful with the method.

DIVINING TWIG
Finding undergrou water with forked twigs is a method that is still used today in places. The twig is stretch out taut in the diviner's hands. For diviners, it twis violently when it is carried over the underground wate

The divi

JAMES HUTTON
Hutton was a Scottish geologist whose interest in agriculture led him to study the fertility of soil. This led him to more wide-ranging observations of the surrounding Scottish countryside. His Plutonist ideas about the origins of rocks being related to volcanic activity came from studies of the volcanic rocks in Edinburgh. This contradicted the Neptunists, who held different views about the origin of rocks (p. 22). It was Hutton's work that gave the first hints of the immensity of geological time.

Small hand ax

Flaked cutting edge

Large hand ax

THE STONE AGE

When people first learned to use the materials from which the Earth is made, stone was their first choice. Some rock types were more suitable than others; they could be worked to a sharp edge that lasted, even when used for heavy tasks such as felling trees. Not all rocks made good tools. Some rocks could not be sharpened, while others were too weak to retain their sharp edge.

Cutting edge used for chopping wood and skinning animals

DIVINING LANDSCAPE

Feng shui is the ancient Chinese practice of landscape divining. The landscape is believed to contain hidden energy. *Feng shui* sees rounded hills as having female characteristics (yin) and rugged mountains as having male characteristics (yang). Along with other elements, such as fire and water, these must all be balanced if there is to be harmony and prosperity.

The compass is consulted

Ch'ing dynasty painting showing *feng shui* compass in use

CHINESE COMPASS

The origins of the *feng shui* compass are unclear. It may have developed from a simple diviner's board, which was used for direction finding, or its origin may be connected with the chess board, since pieces were thrown on to the board as dice. The name *feng shui* means wind and water. In Hong Kong, the *feng shui* diviner is still consulted before any building of significance is built or bought. This ensures that the site, the architectural style, and the purpose of the building are in harmony.

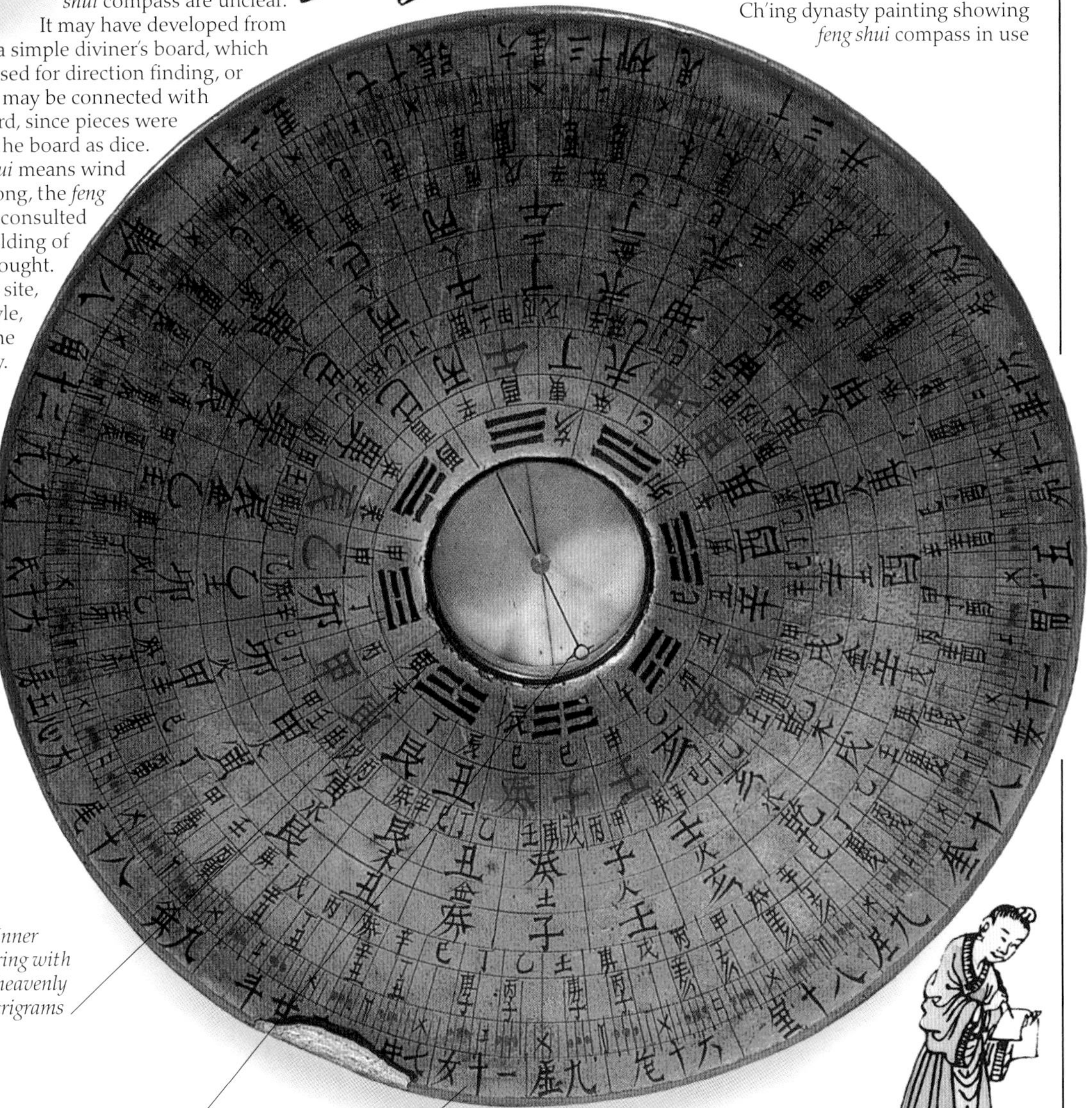

Inner ring with heavenly trigrams

Compass needle

Lacquered wood

NGING HARMONY

ny satisfying buildings throughout world follow the principles of *feng i*. According to *feng shui*, straight es are bad because they allow ergy to rush too forcefully through landscape for its beneficial powers be used. A winding pathway or an dulating wall, as here at Chengde China, brings better harmony h the universe.

The scribe notes the elements in the landscape while measurements are taken

A cocoon of gas

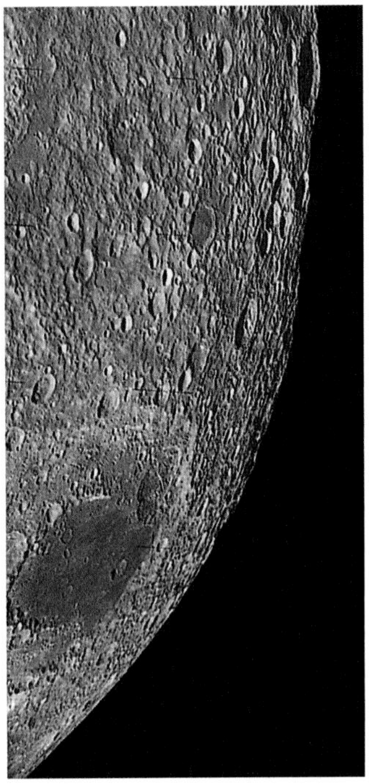

PERPETUAL BLACK SKY
The Moon has no atmosphere surrounding it. This makes its sky black, because there are no atmospheric gases to trap and scatter sunlight that would create a blue or white sky. Because it lacks atmospheric gases, the Moon also has no weather.

THE OUTERMOST PART OF THE EARTH is its shroud of gas, the atmosphere. It extends out at least 600 miles (1,000 km) above the solid surface of the Earth, but three-quarters of this life-sustaining atmosphere is concentrated in the lowest 6 miles (10 km). The atmosphere is a mixture of different gases which together make up air. The most abundant gas in the lower atmosphere is nitrogen, which makes up 78 percent. Oxygen, so vital in supporting animal life on the Earth, makes up about 21 percent. Carbon dioxide, just a small fraction of the total atmosphere, is vital in sustaining plant life; it plays a role in keeping the temperature of the atmosphere steady. Tiny traces of other gases—argon and neon—are clues to the origin of the Earth's atmosphere. The Earth's atmosphere has mostly come from gases spewed out by volcanoes since the Earth began, although some, like oxygen, are a later contribution by living organisms. The layer of the atmosphere closest to the land is called the troposphere. Here, temperature and humidity change rapidly, and the air is turbulent, thus creating weather patterns.

GREEN SLIME
The oxygen in the Earth's atmosphe[re] was created by plantlike organisms th[at] use photosynthesis to make sugar fr[om] carbon dioxide and water, giving ou[t] oxygen. The earliest photosynthesizi[ng] organisms probably looked like these algae, which today grow in ho[t] volcanic springs. Once the algae ha[d] evolved, about 3.6 billion years ago, they began slowly to add oxygen to the atmosphere.

Paralvinella

UNSEEING CREATURES
Some creatures on the Earth exist without atmospheric oxygen. Blind and living in the perpetual darkness of the deep ocean, these sulfide worms have developed an alternative body chemistry to cope with their environment. They get their energy supply from sulfide minerals oozing from hot springs on the ocean floor (p. 38), where temperatures reach 518°F (270°C). Bacteria living nearby take dissolved carbon dioxide from the ocean water and build organic molecules using the hydrogen sulfide from the mineral springs.

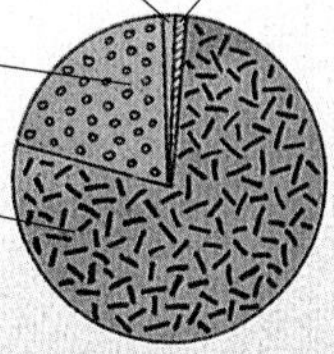

Carbon dioxide
Argon and others
Oxygen
Nitrogen

GASES IN THE ATMOSPHERE
The Earth's atmosphere is unique. If it had formed from gases that are abundant in the solar system, the Earth would have an atmosphere made up mostly of hydrogen and helium, with some methane and ammonia. Instead, processes such as the evolution of bacterial life-forms and plants have created an atmosphere dominated by nitrogen. Another feature of the Earth's atmosphere is that most of its argon is Ar40 (argon 40), from radioactive decay of potassium 40, whereas gases in the solar system are dominated by Ar36 and Ar38.

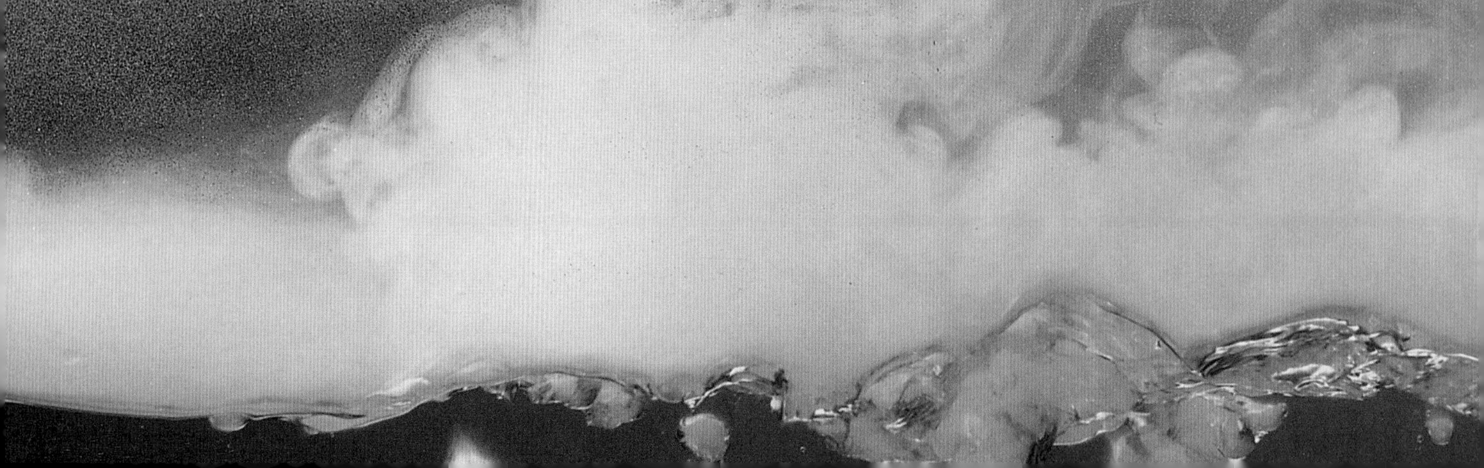

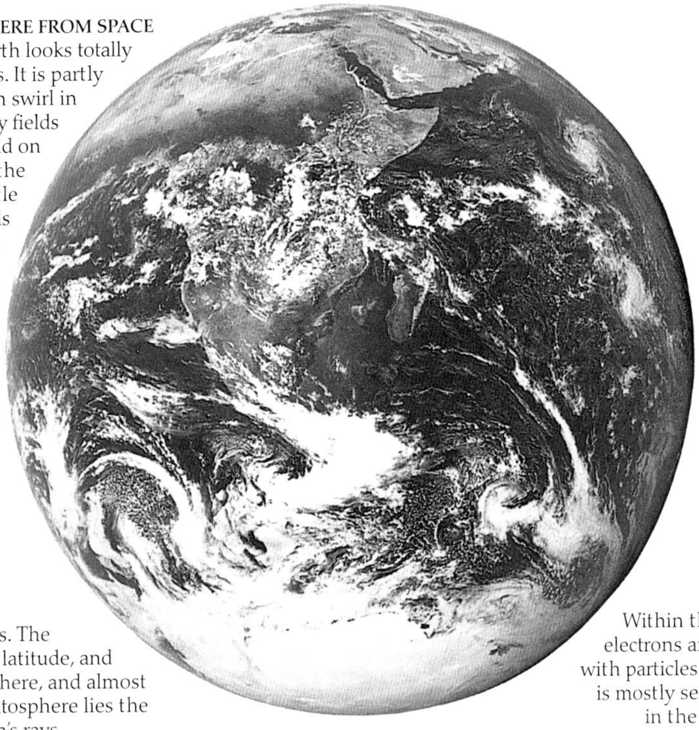

THE ATMOSPHERE FROM SPACE
Viewed from space, the Earth looks totally unlike all the other planets. It is partly shrouded in white clouds, which swirl in patterns, making weather. The gravity fields of small planetary bodies cannot hold on to lightweight molecules of gas, so the Moon, Mercury, and Mars have little atmosphere. Venus, being larger, holds an atmosphere rich in carbon dioxide.

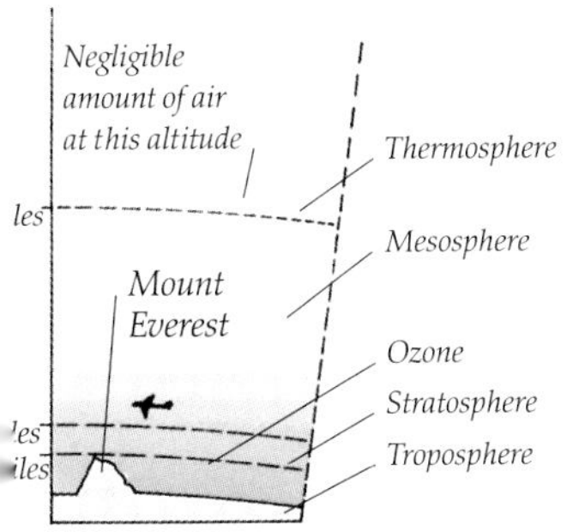

Negligible amount of air at this altitude
Thermosphere
Mesosphere
Mount Everest
Ozone
Stratosphere
Troposphere

ERS OF ATMOSPHERE
e Earth's atmosphere has several layers. The ghts of these layers vary with season, latitude, and e. Weather is confined to the troposphere, and almost clouds are below this level. In the stratosphere lies the portant ozone layer that filters the Sun's rays.

AURORA AUSTRALIS
Within the thermosphere, 180 miles (300 km) up, electrons and protons thrown off by the Sun interact with particles to produce a shimmering light effect. This is mostly seen at polar latitudes. This aurora australis, in the southern hemisphere, was photographed from the space shuttle *Discovery* in 1991.

d hematite
iron oxide)
Black hematite
(an iron oxide)

BANDED IRON
Between about 2 and 3 billion years ago, layers of red and black striped rocks were formed that rarely occur later on in the Earth's history. These are the banded iron formations, where the iron has reacted chemically with oxygen to form oxides. During the time these formed, they must have used up huge amounts of oxygen from the oceanic waters. This proves that at this time algae (p. 10) were rapidly increasing in numbers, making the oceans steadily more oxygen-rich. Oxygen began to escape into the atmosphere as red iron oxide sediments accumulated on land.

FERTILE LAND
The diversity of life that flourishes on the Earth is unique. The Earth's atmosphere gives some protection from harmful space radiation. Its gases provide nourishment for both plants and animals. Winds in the troposphere and ocean currents distribute heat around the world, moderating daily and seasonal temperatures.

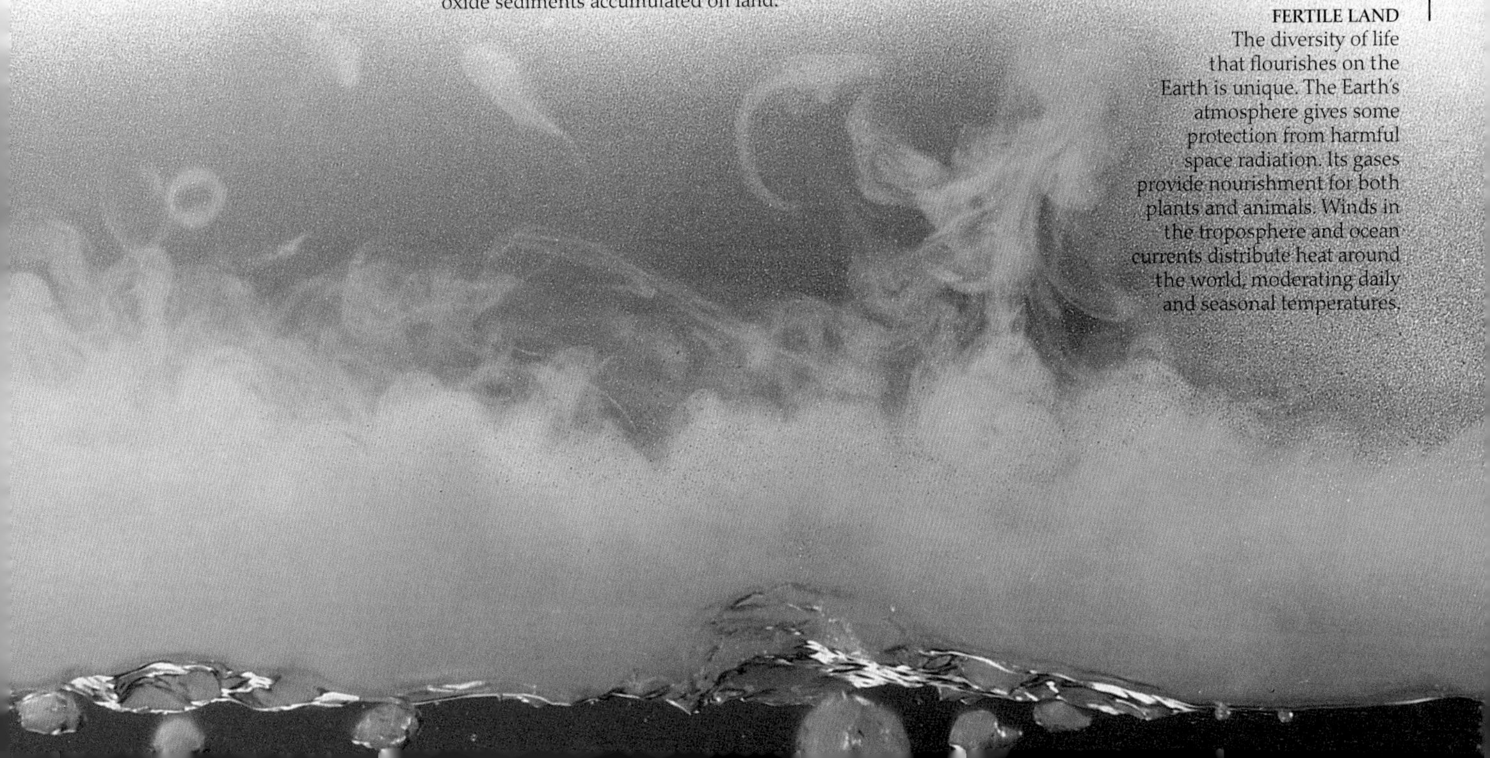

Climate in the past

THE ROLE OF THE SUN
In 1941 the Croatian meteorologist Milutin Milankovitch suggested that changes in the Earth's orbit around the Sun caused long-term changes in climate. He spent many years figuring out how much radiation from the Sun had been received at different latitudes over the last 650,000 years to help prove his theories.

THE EARTH'S CLIMATE HAS CHANGED enormously over geological time. The shapes of the continents have altered and they have moved around relative to the equator and to the poles (pp. 36–37). To find out about these changes, geologists look into the rocks and read them as a kind of history book, going back 4 billion years. The rocks show that places now far from the equator have had baking deserts at times in the past, and that tropical coral reefs flourished on shorelines of what is now Europe. The positions of the continents have an effect on the movement of air masses and on weather patterns. When all the continents were together as Pangaea (pp. 34–35), not much rain fell in the interior, which was largely a desert. The rocks also show that in the last 2 million years glaciers covered large parts of the world (pp. 58–59). Another reason for climate change is the position of the Earth in its orbit in relation to the Sun.

CHANGING POSITIONS
The Earth's orbit is an ellipse—it is sometimes more circular, and sometimes less circular, so that the distance of the Earth from the Sun varies. The changing positions of the Sun and the Moon give an uneven pull on the Earth's bulging Equator. So 11,000 years ago, the northern hemisphere, which then was thick with glacier ice, was nearest the Sun in summer, encouraging the glaciers to melt, helping to bring an end to the Ice Age.

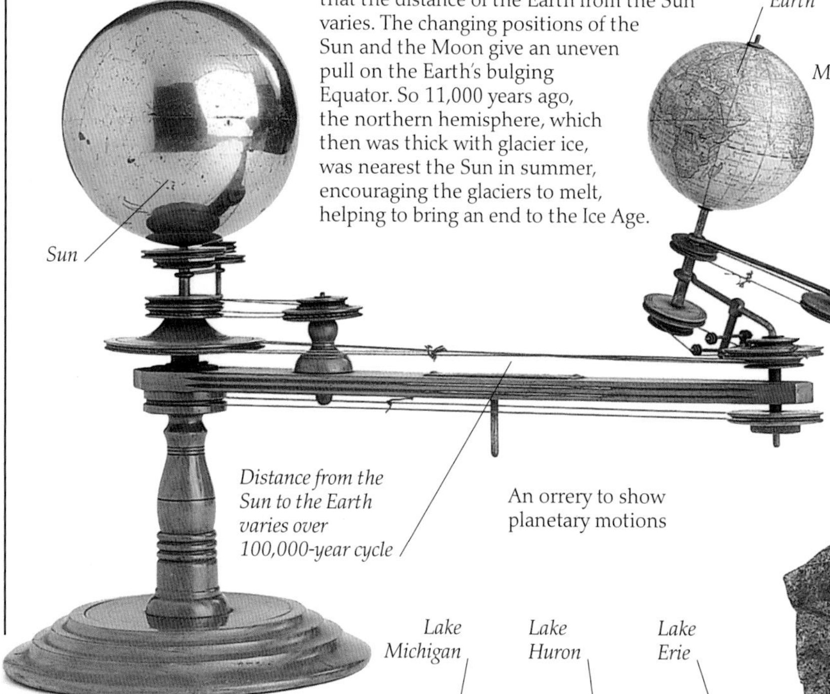

Earth
Moon
Sun
Distance from the Sun to the Earth varies over 100,000-year cycle

An orrery to show planetary motions

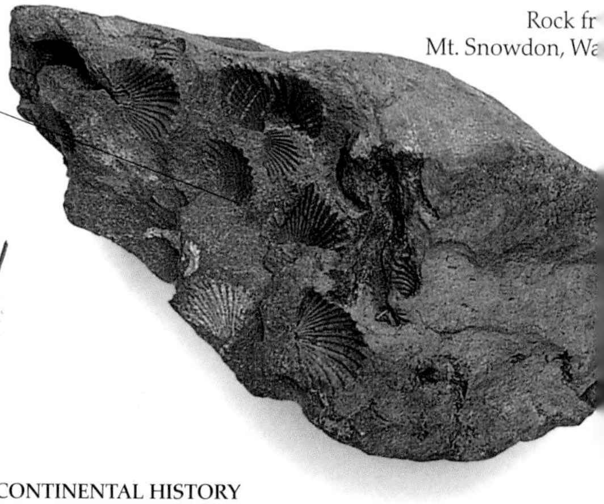

Impression of shell

Rock fr
Mt. Snowdon, Wa

CONTINENTAL HISTORY
Fossils tell us about climate and environment in the past. Se shells found in rocks of high mountains show that marine sediment deposits have been uplifted to form high plateaux and mountain ranges (pp. 46–49). The fossil plant *Glossopte* is found in rocks 350–200 million years old within eac of the southern hemisphe continents. This, along with other evidence, indicates that all the land masses must have been joine together durin this time.

Glossopteris *leaf*
Straight leaf margin

Shale rock from India

ICE-AGE LEGACY
The five Great Lakes of North America owe their origin to changes in glacier ice over the last 14,000 years. The huge weight of the thick sheet of ice pushed down the surface of the land underneath, making a low area. This low region persisted long after the glaciers had melted; the rock was slow to bounce back on release of the pressure (pp. 40–41). As the glacier ice melted, it provided thousands of years' worth of fresh meltwater, which formed as lakes on the low land.

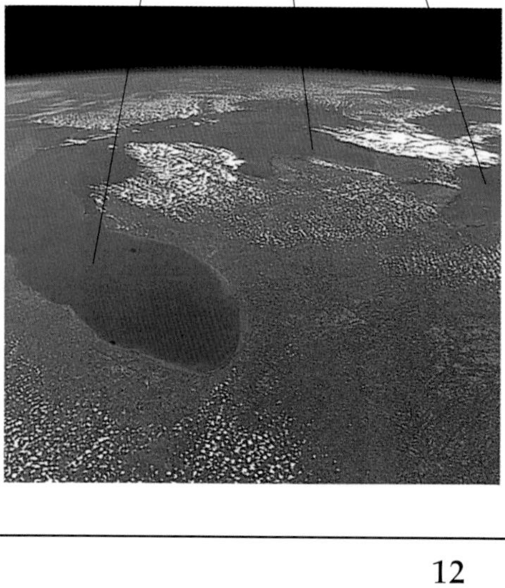

Lake Michigan
Lake Huron
Lake Erie

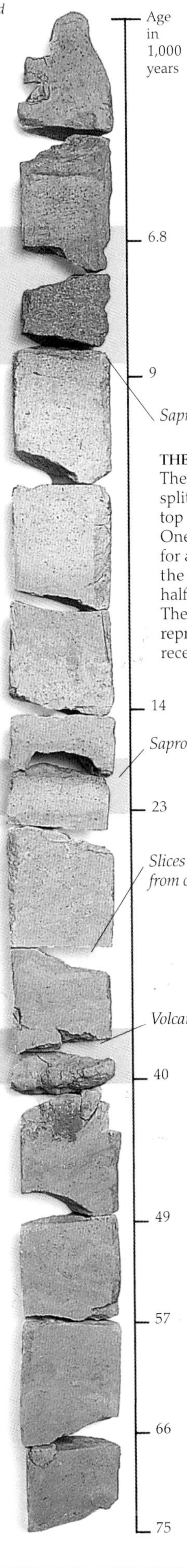

Age in 1,000 years
6.8
9
Sapropel
14
Sapropel
23
Slices taken from core
Volcanic ash
40
49
57
66
75

Investigating a core

One way to find out how climate has changed is to investigate the layers of sediment that have collected on the seafloor. When the climate changed in the past, sea or lake water temperature changed, too. Different types of plants and animals flourished in these varied conditions. When they died, their remains sank and became part of the sediment (pp. 26–27). The fossil remains accumulated in the muds and oozes that formed at that time. To investigate the sediment, a special drilling ship makes a borehole down into the seabed (p. 32) and collects the core from the borehole. This core was taken in the Mediterranean Sea and used to investigate planktonic *Foraminifera* (forams)—tiny marine animals with shells of calcium carbonate.

THE CORE
The core is first split in two from top to bottom. One half is used for analysis, while the matching half is preserved. The top levels represent the most recent sediments.

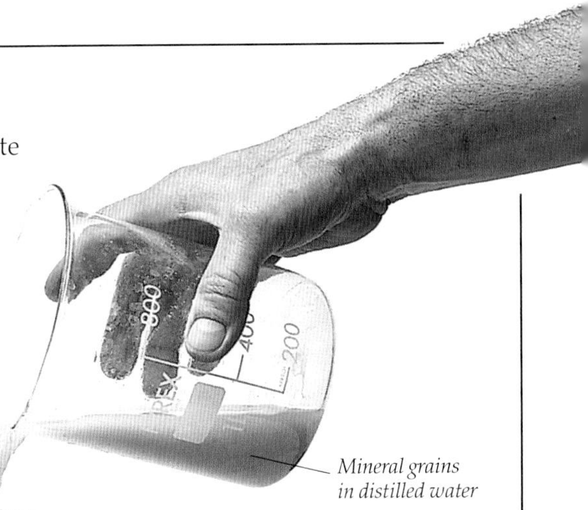

Mineral grains in distilled water

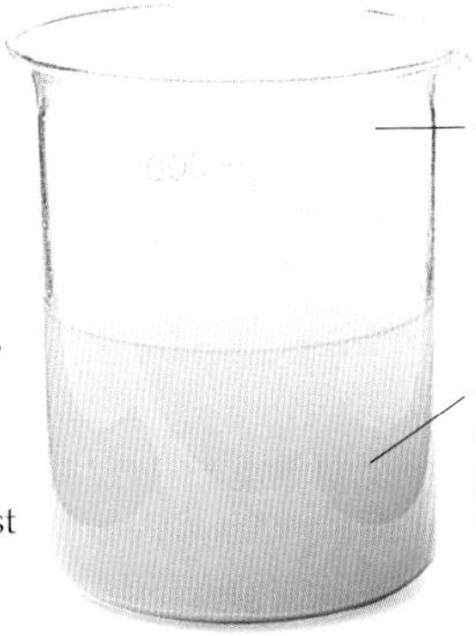

Beaker
Dilute hydrogen peroxide mixture

Mineral grains catch in sieve
Fine mesh sieve

Dried forams

1 BREAKING DOWN THE MATERIAL
The analysis half-core is sampled at 4 in (10 cm) intervals. A small chunk of each sample is weighed and mixed with dilute hydrogen peroxide. The hydrogen peroxide mixture reacts with organic material (soft parts of tiny dead animals, animal droppings, and decaying plants).

2 SIEVING THE MIXTURE
The mineral grains and fossil shells are then washed with distilled water on a fine sieve. The fossils remain on the surface of the sieve and the finer mineral grains pass through.

3 DRYING OFF
The fossils are placed in a warm oven until all moisture evaporates. Meanwhile, the mineral grains are examined. This core showed that most of the sediment grains come from nearby locations—Bulgaria, Turkey, Cyprus, and Greece.

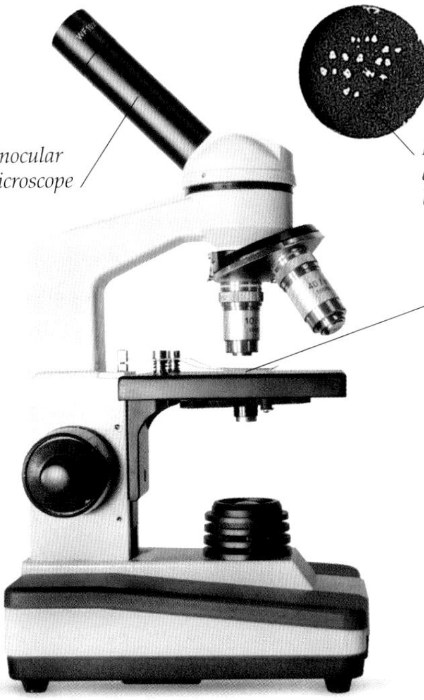

Binocular microscope
Forams arranged by type
Forams

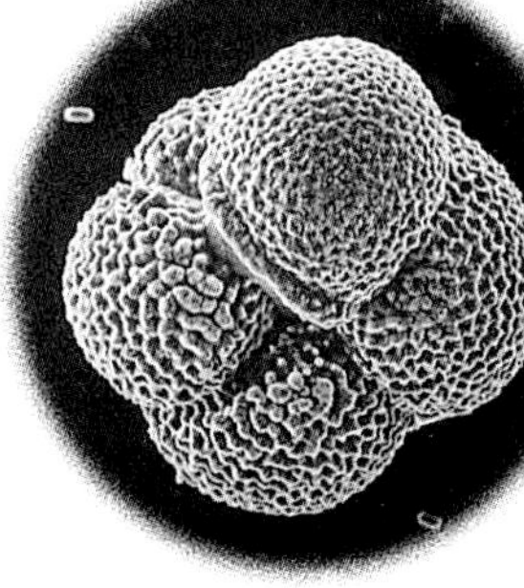

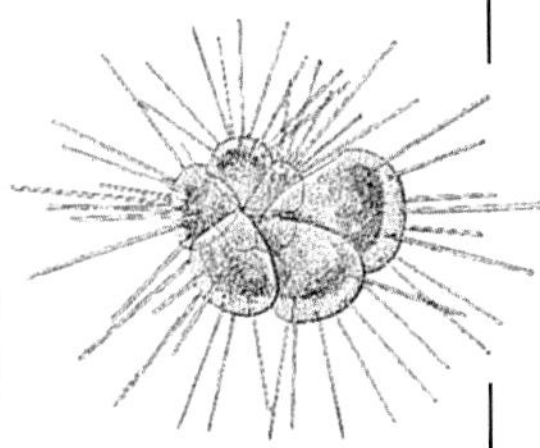

Neogloboquadrina pachyderma engraved as it looked alive (above) and magnified by a scanning electron microscope (left)

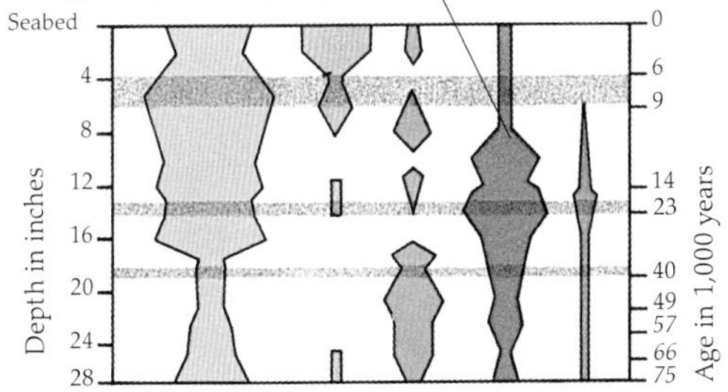

Neogloboquadrina pachyderma
Seabed
Depth in inches
4
8
12
16
20
24
28
Age in 1,000 years
0
6
9
14
23
40
49
57
66
75

4 COUNTING THE SPECIES
The shells of tiny forams can be seen in stereoscopic vision. A scientist identifies the different species and counts each one. The species present, and the relative numbers of each species, are evidence of what the ocean surface temperature was like for each sample of the core.

5 COLLATING THE DATA
Charts are drawn up, showing five species of foram and how the numbers vary at different depths within the core. Some species are more abundant in the warm climatic episodes, representing interglacial periods; others are more abundant when the water was colder, during the cold phases of the Pleistocene Ice Age. Certain climates produced sapropel, a jellylike sludge of plant remains.

Watery planet

Over three-quarters of the Earth's surface is covered by water—it would be more logical to call the planet "Water" instead of "Earth." Even with the continents scattered around as they are today, one great ocean dominates half the globe. Of the rain that falls on the land, just over one-third runs off into rivers and is quickly returned to the ocean. The other two-thirds soaks into the soil and underlying rock and remains for years or even tens of thousands of years as ground water. It is ground water that nourishes springs and wells and keeps rivers flowing in times of drought. All water is involved in a never-ending flow from ocean to atmosphere to rivers to underground rocks, always returning eventually to the ocean. This great journey is called the water cycle. Understanding the way in which water moves from one place to another is the study of hydrology, and someone who looks specifically at the movement of underground water is a hydrogeologist.

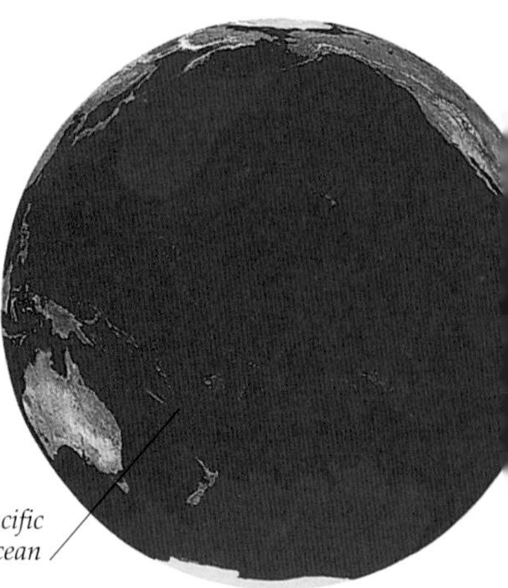

Pacific Ocean

BLUE PLANET

Viewed from a satellite above the Pacific Oce the Earth appears to be almost completely covered in water. A few chains of islands dc the watery surface. The Pacific is so big tha all the land area of the Earth could fit into it. The oceans are much deeper on average than the land is high.

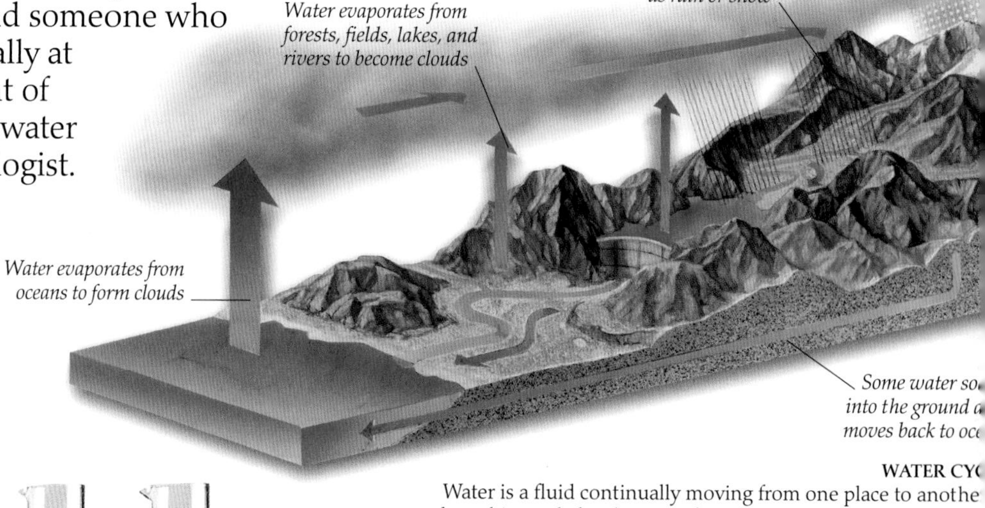

Clouds rise and cool over land and drop moisture as rain or snow
Water evaporates from forests, fields, lakes, and rivers to become clouds
Water evaporates from oceans to form clouds
Some water so into the ground a moves back to oc

WATER CY

Water is a fluid continually moving from one place to anothe does this partly by changing from liquid to vapor and back ag The Sun's heat warms the ocean water near the surface, and so molecules of water are heated enough to evaporate (p. 16). Th energetic molecules escape from the ocean and become water va that collects in clouds. When clouds are cooled, they can no lon hold water as vapor, so drops condense and fall as rain and sn Because of the distribution of land and ocean, most rain falls strai back into the ocean to repeat the cycle. Some rain falls on land a is used by plants and animals. Some gathers in lakes and rivers, o to run downhill into the ocean once more. Some rainfall over la takes longer to return to the ocean; it travels slowly throu tiny pores and cracks in underground ro

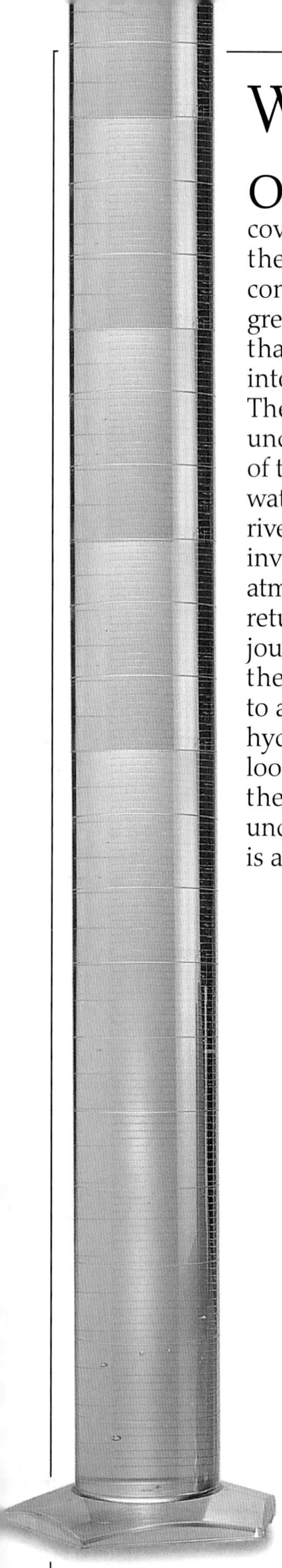

Ocean water 94%

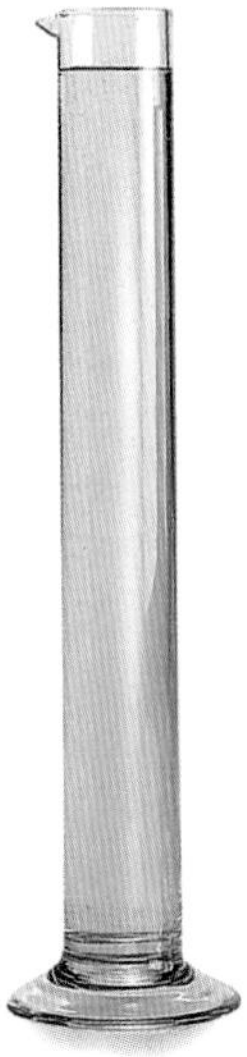

Ground water 4.34%

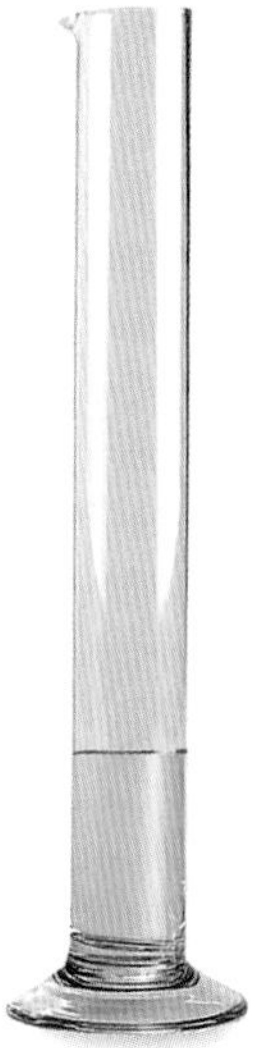

Ice caps and glaciers 1.65%

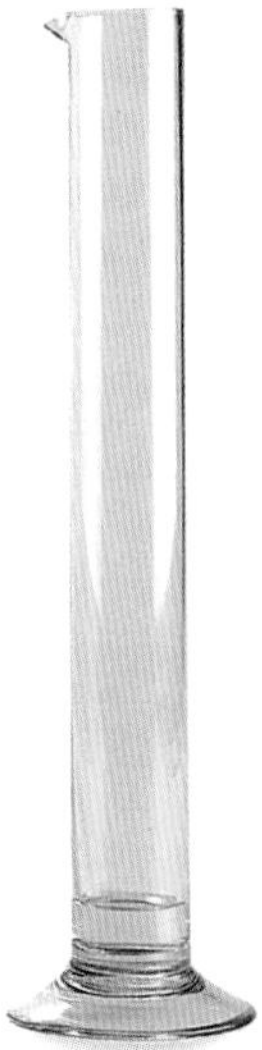

Rivers and lakes 0.01%

Water vapor

QUANTITIES OF WATER

Most of the world's water is salty. Less than 6 percent accounts for all the freshwater in rivers and lakes, the water underground in rocks, and the moisture in the atmosphere. Some freshwater is temporarily locked up in ice caps and glaciers. At the end of the last ice age melting ice raised global sea level by hundreds of feet. If the world climate continues to warm over future centuries, the remaining ice could melt and raise global sea level again by several hundred feet.

TY WATER
concentration of salt in
water is much greater than that
he human body, so drinking
water actually increases thirst
leads to dehydration. How
ch salt there is in seawater is
wn by boiling it until all the water
evaporated. Some white crystals are left. These
the mixture that makes seawater salty. Seawater
es in how salty it is, depending on how much rain
locally, on the saltiness of the rivers nearby, on
rate of evaporation, and on the depth of the
water from which the sample was taken.

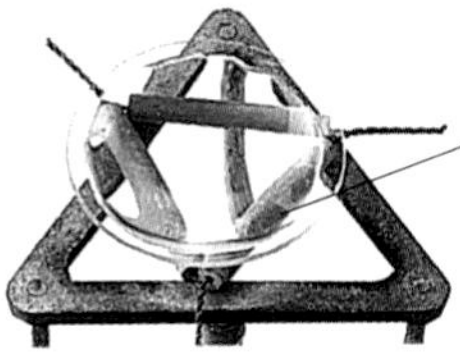
Salt water

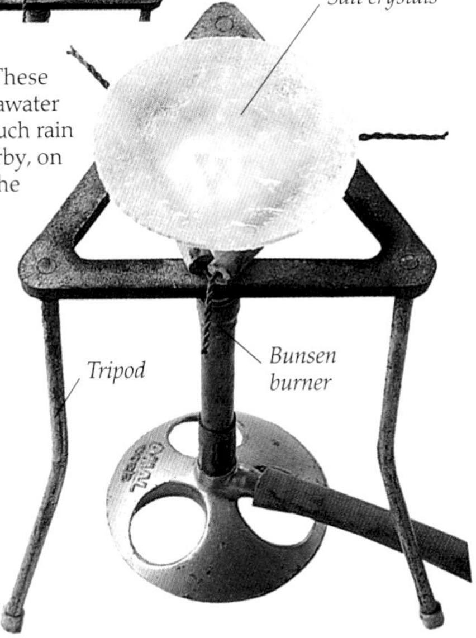
Salt crystals
Tripod
Bunsen burner

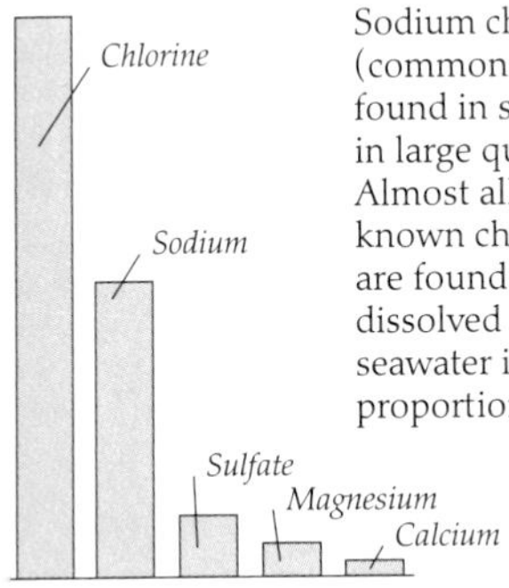
Chlorine
Sodium
Sulfate
Magnesium
Calcium

SEAWATER
Sodium chloride (common salt) is found in seawater in large quantities. Almost all the known chemicals are found dissolved in seawater in some proportion.

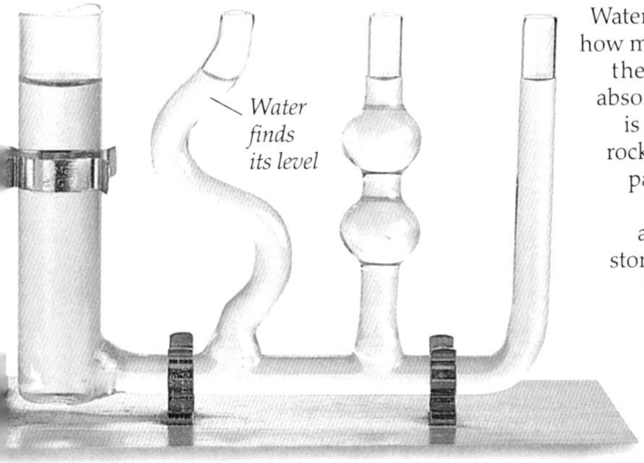
Water finds its level

A LEVEL
oceans are interconnected,
sea level is fairly constant all the
y around the Earth. This
ecause, being a liquid, water
ws downhill to the lowest
ce, and then finds its level
a local area. Inland seas and
es are not connected to the
rld oceans, so their levels
y vary widely. Some are
ove global sea level, others,
h as the Dead Sea in Israel,
below it. Differences
gravity and changes in
nospheric pressure and
tides cause bulges
d depressions in the
face of the oceans.

ROCK AND WATER
Water soaks into some rock; how much water depends on the rock. A rock layer that absorbs water into its pores is made up of permeable rock. It allows the water to pass through and it may become an aquifer. An aquifer acts as a natural storage reservoir for water. Impermeable rocks do not allow water to pass through.

Aquifer water may have some minerals dissolved in it from the rock

The properties of water

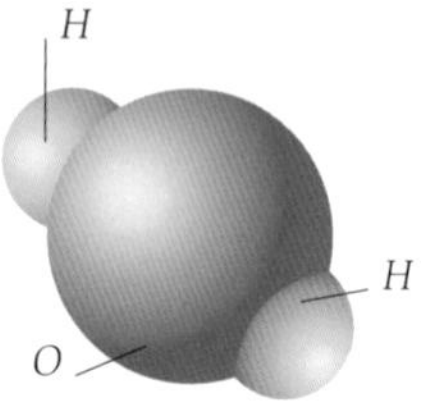

H
H
O

UNITS OF WATER
Water is made up of two elements—oxygen and hydrogen. Its molecules bind together to form aggregates of water molecules, with a special bond called the hydrogen bond. This causes the molecules to join together, so that at room temperature, water forms droplets rather than floating around as a gas.

WATER IS AN UNUSUAL LIQUID because of the way its molecules are bonded together. One effect of this bonding is the unusual density of water. Most substances occupy a smaller space—they become more dense—as they are cooled. However, water is most dense at 39.2°F (4°C). Below that temperature, its density becomes less. Ice at 32°F (0°C) is less dense than water at 32°F. This is why ice floats on water. Water takes a huge amount of heat to transform it from its liquid state into a gas, and from its solid state, ice, into a liquid. The equable temperature on the Earth is largely maintained by these unusual characteristics of water. Water also has high surface tension, which helps in making raindrops in the atmosphere and in the way water is able to travel through rocks and soil. Water is a solvent; it dissolves a great many substances relatively easily. Its ability to do this affects how rocks are weathered (pp. 50–51), since some of the chemical elements that make up rocks go into solution during weathering.

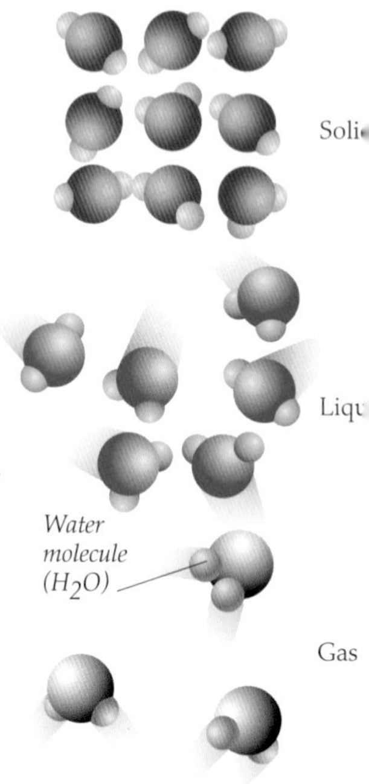

Soli
Liqu
Water molecule (H_2O)
Gas

SOLID, LIQUID, AND G
Most substances pack together into a regu arrangement when they are in a solid state. As liquid, the ordered arrangement breaks down, a the molecules are more spaced out. With more heat, t spacing gets greater, until eventually molecules are so apart that the substance becomes a gas. As water cooled to 39.2°F (4°C), or cold water is heated 39.2°F , the molecules pack together in more economical way, so that th occupy less space. This gives wat its maximum density this temperatu

MAKING RAINDROPS
The surface tension of water is the ability of the surface to shrink and "wrap around" the water so that it holds the contents together. The clingy wetness of water is also a result of the surface tension. The force of the surface pulling to hold the water together is enough to allow water to soak up and wet a towel or filter paper when they are dipped into the water.

Water remains in droplets

ırve on
ɾface
water
een dye
ded
water

RAFT SPIDER

When a raft spider (*Dolomedes fimbriatus*) walks on a pond, its weight and the way it is distributed over the feet is less than the pulling-together effect of water's surface tension, so the raft spider floats. The water surface curves down around its feet. This surface tension effect is how water wets things. As its surface pulls together, it surrounds fibers or grains of rock or soil with which it comes into contact.

Egg sinks in tap water
Egg floats in salty water

CAPILLARY ACTION

If a thin tube stands upright in water, the water will rise up inside the tube. There is an upward curve of the water surface where the water touches the tube. The thinner the tube, the higher the water rises, as surface tension pulls the curved surface together. Water soaks into soil and rocks and moves down under the force of gravity. However, water also travels up through rocks by this capillary action. The curved surface always pulls together as the water envelops each tiny grain of rock in turn. Water can therefore be drawn up through soil and rock and evaporated at the surface (p. 14).

FLOATING EGGS

The density of water changes when it has salt dissolved in it. An egg sinks in freshwater, which means the egg has a density greater than that of the water. Salty water is more dense than freshwater, and when the amount of saltiness—the salinity—is high enough, the egg floats. The varying density of seawater is one of the factors that drives the water currents that circulate water in the oceans.

80
76
60
50
40
Weight
Flotation bulb

Hydrometer

MEASURING DENSITY

A hydrometer is an instrument that measures the density of a liquid. It is floated upright in the liquid, sinking more deeply into less dense liquids. Weights are attached to it and the reading taken. This one was used to measure the alcohol content of drinks for assessing the amount of tax payable.

LIMESTONE CAVES

The hydrogen and oxygen that go to make up water are bonded together in such a way that the molecule has a positive charge at one end and a negative charge at the other. This makes it easy for water to attract other charged substances, and it does this by dissolving them. It dissolves the rock limestone to make caves. Later, the dissolved chemicals may become stalagmites and stalactites (p. 51).

Limestone caves at Lascaux in France

Acid
Carbon dioxide gas is given off
Calcium carbonate chips

ACID RAIN

Pure water is neither acid nor alkaline. Indicator paper held in pure or distilled water shows that it is neutral. Rainwater is always acid, because it contains carbon dioxide. As raindrops fall through the atmosphere, they dissolve some carbon dioxide from the air. This makes the rain a weak acid. In this experiment, carbon dioxide gas is made by adding acid to calcium carbonate chips. The gas is passed into distilled water, which then becomes acid, as shown by the indicator paper. Acid rainwater is a weathering agent; it can dissolve limestone—although slowly.

Indicator paper shows neutral
Distilled water

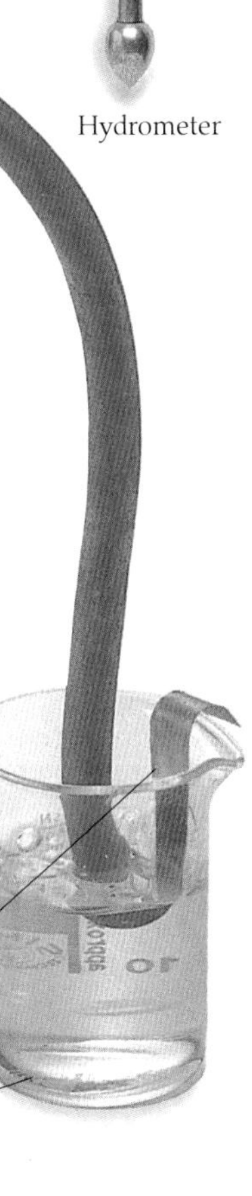

Indicator paper shows slight acidity
Carbonic acid

LOUIS AGASSIZ (1807–1873)
In 1837, Swiss-American zoologist Agassiz put forward the idea that northern Europe had once been covered with glaciers. These glaciers had carried the boulders, which littered the Swiss mountain valleys, made of rocks similar to those rock types found higher up the valleys.

Realms of ice

MANY OF THE WORLD'S HIGH MOUNTAIN RANGES still have glaciers (pp. 58–59). Both glaciers and ice sheets were much more extensive during the cold glacial phases of the last two million years. Now the Earth is believed to be in an interglacial period, with Greenland and Antarctica the only extensively ice-covered lands—leftovers from the last cold phase. The Antarctic ice sheet probably came into existence 35 million years ago, when Antarctica broke away from the other land masses (pp. 30–31). This allowed free circulation of oceanic currents around Antarctica, isolating it from the warmth of the tropical oceanic waters (p. 33). The water to make ice comes from snow that falls and is compacted. This snow comes from water vapor that has evaporated from the oceans (p. 14), so sea level drops. When glaciers and ice sheets melt, sea level rises again.

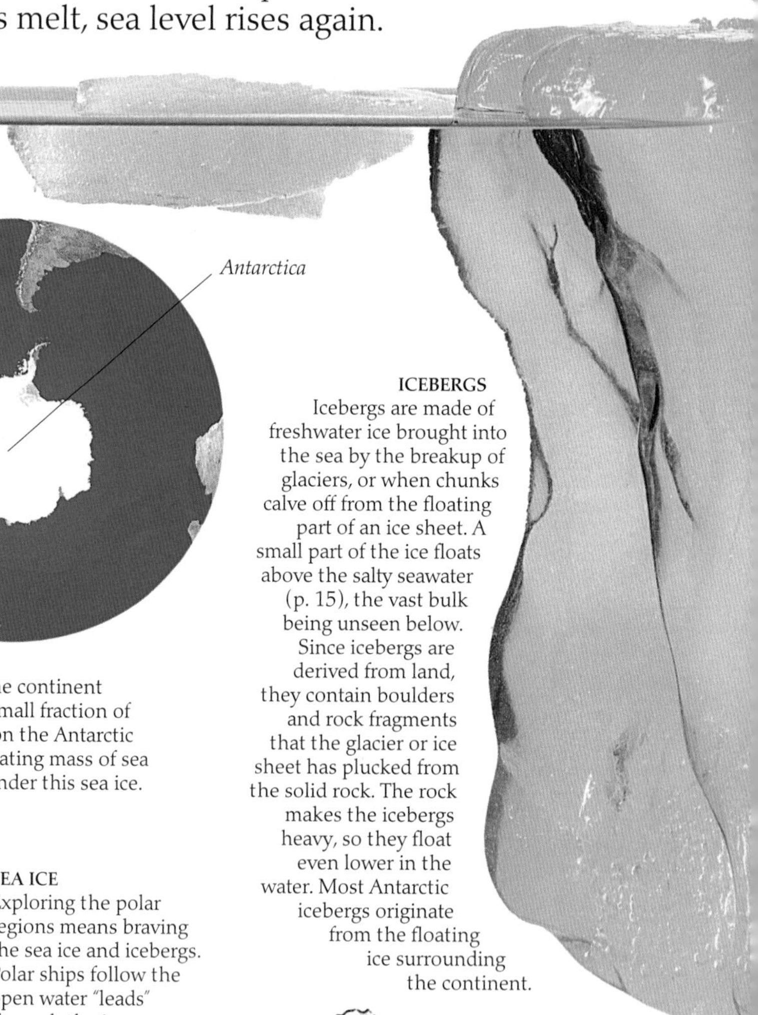

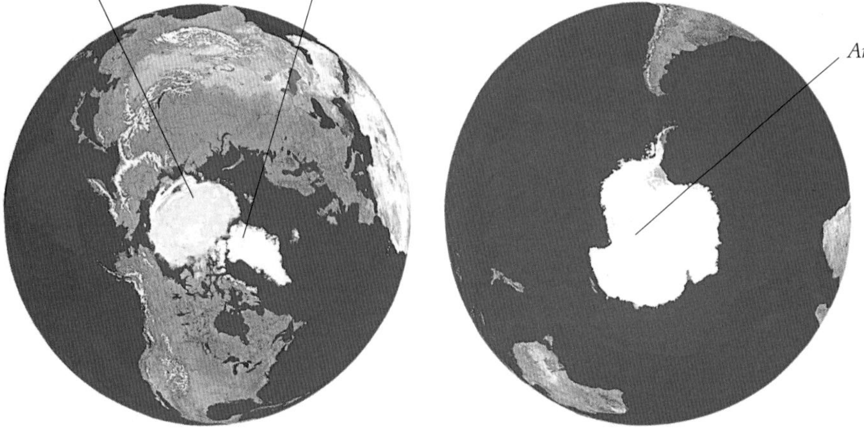

Arctic ice
Greenland
Antarctica

POLAR ICE
The South Pole is surrounded by thick ice that covers the continent of Antarctica to an average depth of 1½ miles (2.5 km). A small fraction of the Antarctic ice sheet extends beyond the land and floats on the Antarctic Ocean. By contrast, the North Pole has no land. It is a thin floating mass of sea ice—it is possible to travel by submarine to the North Pole under this sea ice.

ICEBERGS
Icebergs are made of freshwater ice brought into the sea by the breakup of glaciers, or when chunks calve off from the floating part of an ice sheet. A small part of the ice floats above the salty seawater (p. 15), the vast bulk being unseen below. Since icebergs are derived from land, they contain boulders and rock fragments that the glacier or ice sheet has plucked from the solid rock. The rock makes the icebergs heavy, so they float even lower in the water. Most Antarctic icebergs originate from the floating ice surrounding the continent.

SEA ICE
Exploring the polar regions means braving the sea ice and icebergs. Polar ships follow the open water "leads" through the ice. Their hulls are specially strengthened to help batter their way through, and also to the hulls from crushing if the ice should freeze around them. The floating ice of both hemispheres is called pack ice. The amount of ice varies from summer to winter.

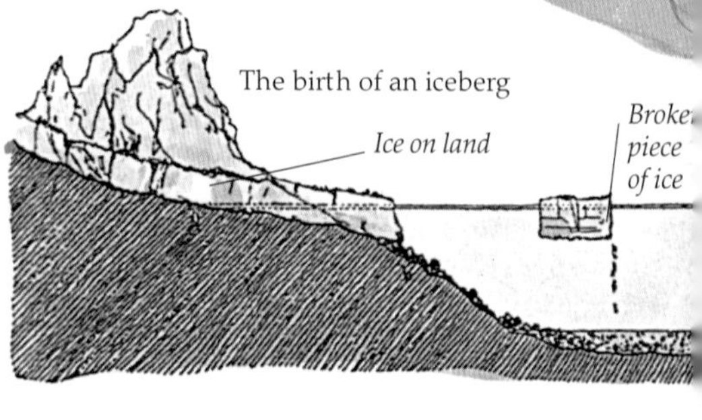

Ice on land
Broke
piece
of ice

The birth of an iceberg

ALUM
SULPHUR
FLUATE LIME

Chemicals for use with rock specimens

Cupel with spirit burner for heating chemicals

TT, THE SCIENTIST

tain Robert Scott (1868–1912) died returning from rek to the South Pole. He is less well-known for his ntific work during the trip. His equipment included portable chemistry laboratory, which enabled him ork on the rock samples collected by the edition as he traveled.

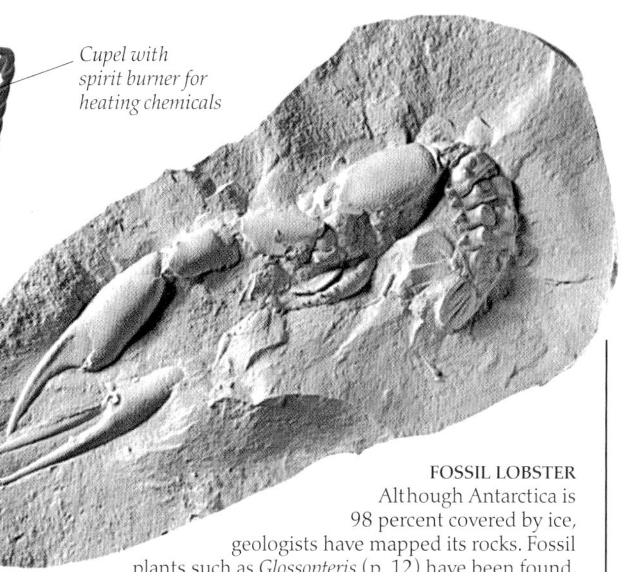

FOSSIL LOBSTER

Although Antarctica is 98 percent covered by ice, geologists have mapped its rocks. Fossil plants such as *Glossopteris* (p. 12) have been found, and more recently many crustacean fossils have been uncovered, some of which are new species not found elsewhere. This fossil lobster from Upper Cretaceous rocks is about 80 million years old.

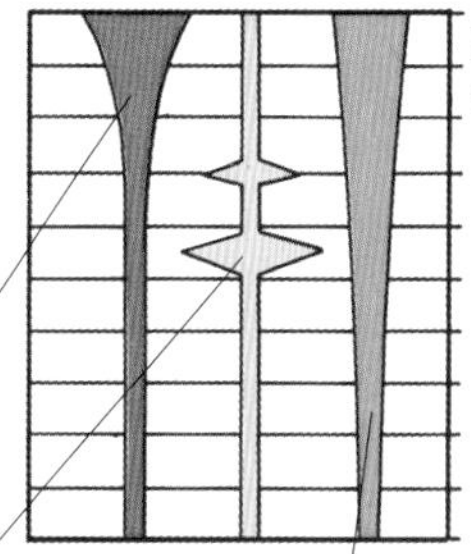
Radio-
active
fallout
Sulfates
Lead
Present
day
Time in 30-year cycles
Nuclear tests (1950s)
Eruption of Krakatau (1883)
Industrial Revolution (1750)

ANALYZING ICE CORES

This ice core was drilled from the polar ice sheet and returned to the laboratory for tests. Minute amounts are taken at regular intervals and analyzed to find out more about the atmosphere and climate of the past, in the same way a sediment core from the sea floor is analyzed (p. 13). The ice is melted naturally in sterile conditions, so that no pollutants from the new environment contaminate it. The results are collated on a chart to show the levels of atmospheric gases and chemicals present in the snow.

INVESTIGATING POLAR ICE

laciologists work in dug-out laboratories in the ice. The olar ice sheet preserves snowfall from the past within its layers. Compressed by more snow above, the layers get hinner the more deeply they are buried (p. 59). Trapped ithin the solid ice are bubbles of atmospheric gases and ces of substances from the atmosphere. Therefore, an ice ore may hold trapped volcanic dust from major volcanic eruptions, nitric acid from the outer atmosphere, as well as radioactive isotopes from nuclear testing.

The building blocks

GOLD IN NATURE
Gold is both an element and a mineral. It is found almost pure in nature where it may be in veins in rocks. The most pure natural gold is 99 percent pure. For commercial purposes, it is often alloyed with silver. Gold forms cubic crystals and has a bright metallic luster. It is very heavy, but not hard; it can easily be cut with a knife.

OVER ONE HUNDRED CHEMICAL ELEMENTS combine to make up all matter. An element contains only one kind of atom, but atoms from different elements can join together to make a variety of substances called compounds. They do this by joining together (bonding) in different ways to make molecules. A few of the elements make up almost all of the types of naturally occurring compounds called minerals. These minerals make up rocks. Most rocks in the Earth's crust are composed of only eight of the chemical elements—oxygen, silicon, aluminum, iron, calcium, magnesium, sodium, and potassium. Two of these elements, silicon and oxygen, combine in silicates, which make up 75 percent of the Earth's rocks. Most minerals are crystalline—the atoms that make up the crystals are arranged in an orderly fashion. It is the job of the mineralogist to understand what minerals are, where they are to be found, and what they can be used for.

SILICON LOCKET
The chemical elemen
silicon does not occur
nature. Silicon is alwa
found as a silicate in
combination with oxyg
and it takes a lot of
chemical energy to
separate out the silico
from the oxygen in a
laboratory. When it w
first separated, silicon
was considered an exo
substance. This piece w
mounted in a locket.
Today, silicon is
made commercially f
the electronics industr
where it is the raw
material for the microc

New Mexico

WHITE SANDS DESERT
This white sand is made of one mineral, gypsum, which has been weathered by wind (pp. 50–51). The composition of the mineral is calcium, in combination with sulfur and oxygen, to make the chemical calcium sulfate. The crystals of calcium sulfate in nature contain some water, and this combination goes to make up the mineral gypsum. Crystals of gypsum are soft and can be scratched with a fingernail. Gypsum forms crystals that are uncolored and transparent, and sometimes white.

ELEMENTS IN THE EARTH'S CRUST
The crust, or lithosphere, is the outermost solid layer on the Earth's surface (pp. 6–7). Oxygen atoms are so large that almost all of the Earth's crust is made of them with the other elements just filling in the spaces between. Silicon atoms are small and fit happily between four oxygen atoms. Therefore, the most abundant elements in the crust are those that readily combine with the relatively lightweight silicon and oxygen to make silicates. These elements fit into the physical spaces in the silicate framework and make up the common rock-forming minerals such as feldspars, pyroxenes, amphiboles, olivines, and micas.

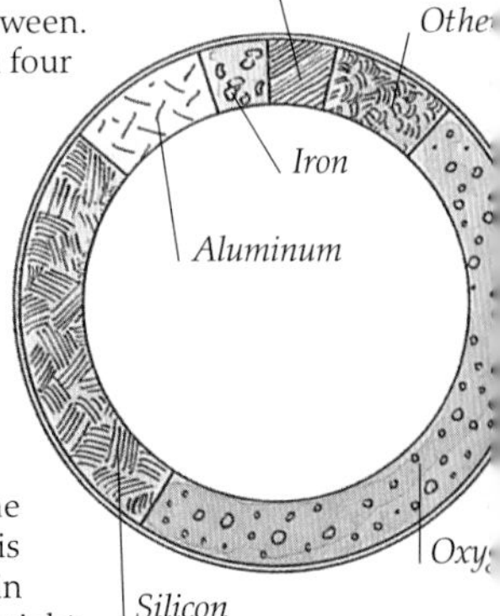
Calcium
Iron
Aluminum
Silicon

Elements in the Earth's crust

DIFFERENT SILICATES
Two very different silicates are talc, familiar as the slippery white cosmetic powder, and beryl. Talc is a silicate of magnesium, crystallized with water in its structure. Beryl comes in various colors; the bright green variety in hard, clear crystals is the highly prized gemstone, emerald. Beryl is a silicate with aluminum in combination with the much rarer chemical element, beryllium.

Beryl

Talc

SILICATES
Silicon and oxygen combine together to form the mineral quartz, and this commonly appears as sand. In silicates, the silicon atoms are each surrounded by four oxygen atoms, but the oxygen may be shared with neighboring silicons. In this way the framework of silicates is made.

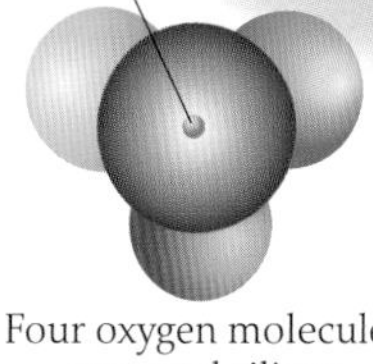
Si

Four oxygen molecules surround silicon

elling minerals apart

lcite, gypsum, and quartz look alike at first nce. All three may come as colorless, transparent stals. All are used in industry in different ways, it is important to be able to distinguish one m the other. Minerals are differentiated by ir appearance, their color, and whether they transparent (an image can be read through em), translucent (let light through), or aque (no light goes into the crystal). Other portant properties are the hardness, the ter, the streak (the color of the powder y make), the density, and the crystal m and shape. More sophisticated tests y be done in a laboratory (p. 23).

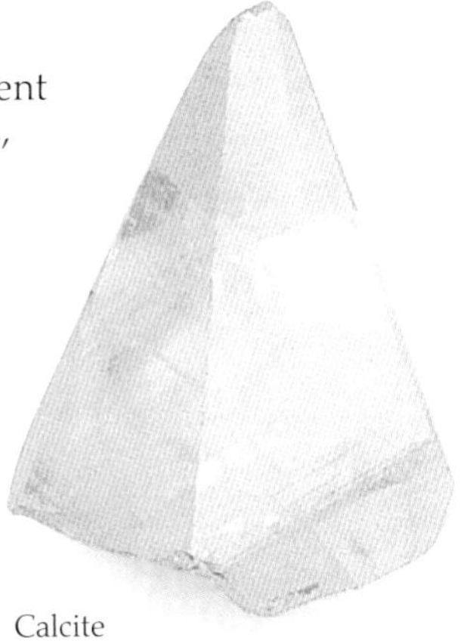

Calcite

Gypsum

Quartz

ICH MINERAL?
determine the minerals piece of rock, a logist first looks at rock through a hand s to check for crystal pe, texture, luster, and or. The next test would bably be the acid test.

ACID TEST
Dilute hydrochloric acid ropped on to the area ng tested. Carbonate ks effervesce (fizz) to give carbon dioxide gas when y meet acid. This ntifies calcite.

Acid is dropped on to the rock

Calcite is a carbonate rock so it fizzes with acid

Rock containing calcite, gypsum, and quartz

HARDNESS TEST
The hardness of nerals is generally asured against a Mohs e, where talc is 1 (the test), and diamond is the hardest material own. A steel penknife is d here to do the test. el has a hardness of und 6, so quartz, at a ater hardness of 7 on Mohs scale, is not atched by a knife, but cite and gypsum are. psum is softer than cite, so the penknife atches it easily. Gypsum o soft it can be atched with a fingernail rdness of 2).

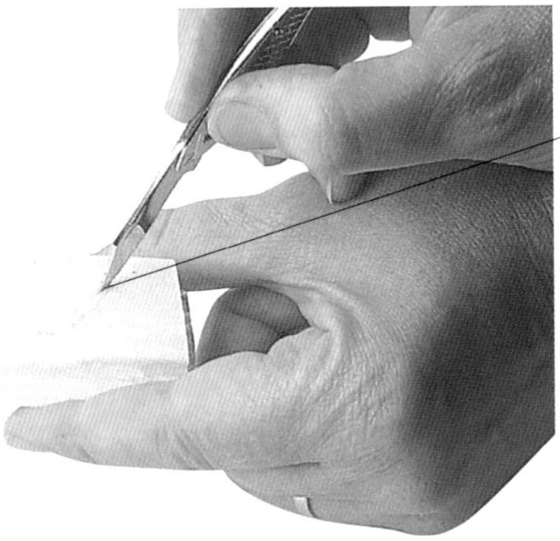

Steel penknife scratches the gypsum

FINDING QUARTZ
Another useful stance for hardness ing is window glass on the Mohs scale). cite is softer than ndow glass (it has a dness of just 3), so it not scratch the glass. ither will gypsum, at n the scale. Quartz he only one of the ee that scratches the ss. The hardness tests firm the findings on three minerals.

Quartz scratches the window glass

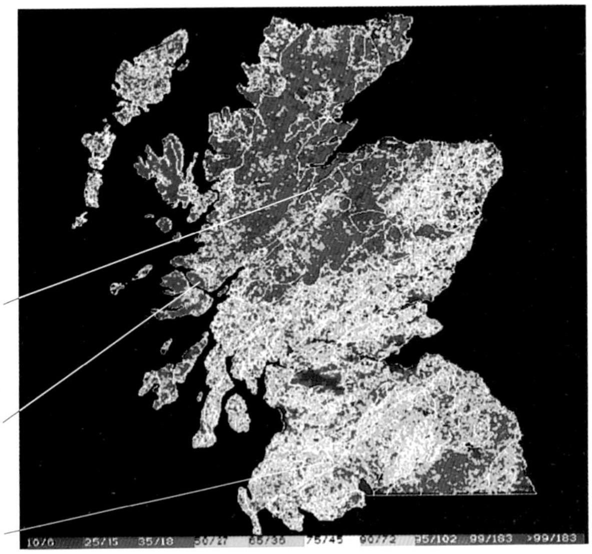

Blue—low copper concentrations

Red—high copper concentrations

Yellow—no suitable data

COPPER CONCENTRATIONS IN SCOTLAND
The amount of various minerals in stream sediments is estimated by taking one sample every kilometer. The results are stored on a computer, and are shown on a map. This map can show concentrations of copper and can be used for mineral exploration and for environmental reasons to check for contamination or pollution. Here, high levels of copper are shown in dark red. The 60-million-year-old lavas of the Inner Hebrides Islands are high in copper, and so are granite regions in the Highlands. Copper also shows up high in industrial areas, where there is no relationship to the underlying rocks; the concentration is the direct result of human activity.

Investigating rocks

Neptune—the Roma
god of the sea

THE FIRST SYSTEMATIC BOOK ON MINERALOGY was written by Agricola (p. 8) in the 16th century. Written in Latin, it was called *De Natura Fossilium*. The word "fossil" then meant "things dug up," and included chiefly minerals and rocks. Agricola based his writings on his own observations, rather than using the speculative or hopeful reasoning that had characterized the writings of the ancient Greeks, and later, the alchemists. In the 18th century, during the Age of Enlightenment, many thinkers were encouraged to contemplate the origin of the Earth and of rocks. A controversy raged between the Neptunists, led by Abraham Werner, and the Plutonists, who believed the origin of some rocks was undoubtedly volcanic, led by James Hutton (p. 8). Europe's scientists were divided into two camps. Toward the end of the 18th century, travel became easier, allowing scientists to observe directly many different types of rocks in different places. In 1830, Charles Lyell (p. 62) published his influential work, *Principles of Geology*. This book influenced other geologists, who responded to Lyell's theories about the slow, gradual nature of the Earth's processes.

JAMES DANA
James Dana (1813–95) was an American geologist best known for his *System of Mineralogy* (1837). He suggested that landscapes were shaped by the ongoing forces of weathering and erosion. His predecessors had imagined that sudden catastrophic events, such as earthquakes, were responsible.

ROCKS FROM WATER
Abraham Werner (1749–1817) was a German geologist wh put forward the ideas of Neptunism. The Neptunists opposed the Plutonists (p. 8). Neptunists believed that the chemicals tha made up rocks had be dissolved in the ocean waters, and all rocks, including basalt, had come out of this solut Werner's fame spread from the eloquence of personal teachings an the dedicat work of students

Abraham
Werner

Geologists in the field

Geologists fall into many categories such as palaeontologists, petrologists, and geochemists, but they all study the Earth, and the place to start is in the rocks. In the field, geologists record their observations in notebooks, take photographs, and collect specimens. The specimens are labeled and wrapped for transport back to the laboratory.

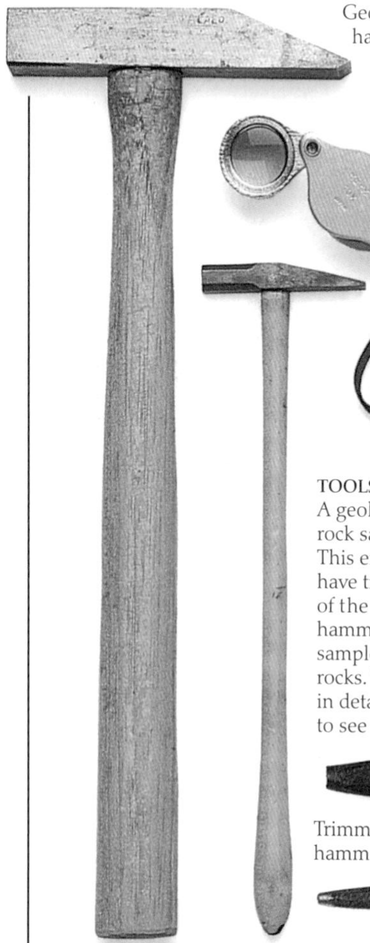

Geological
hammer

Hand lens

Trimming
hammer

TOOLS OF THE TRADE
A geologist uses a hammer to break off rock samples fresh from solid bedrock. This ensures that the samples collected have truly come from the solid rocks of the place being mapped. The small hammer is used for trimming rock samples. A chisel helps in splitting rocks. The hand lens is used to look in detail at the texture of rock, and to see if any fossils are present.

Wide-ended chisel

Pointed chisel

SMITH'S MAP (1819)
The first geological maps were published at the beginning of the 19th century. In 1815, William Smith (p. 26) published the first geological map of Britain. These maps, such as this 1819 map by Smith, show mountains, roads, and other relief features, as well as the different rocks that appear at the surface; the different colors show the different ages of the rocks.

›ERALS IN ROCKS

›oarse-grained granite ws the mineral ›ns that it is ›nposed of. Even ›h the naked eye, feldspars can be ›ly spotted. Feldspars ›ally have sharp crystal lines because they ›tallized first in the ›ling magma (p. 25). ›ing the spaces in between, ›ause it crystallized later, is ›yish glassy quartz. Mica is ›aky mineral, which shows ›as bright spangles because ›ts high reflectivity.

Mica

Quartz

Feldspar

Quartz
Mica
Feldspar
Coarse-grained granite

CONTACT GONIOMETER

The orderly arrangement of atoms inside crystals is unique to each mineral. The internal pattern shows specific angles between the faces on the outside of the crystal. These angles can be measured with a contact goniometer. Most crystals are far too small for use with such a cumbersome measuring instrument, so some other method, such as X-rays, is needed to tell crystals apart. Crystal faces also have markings on them that are distinctive. These might be fine lines or striations, or triangle-shaped markings.

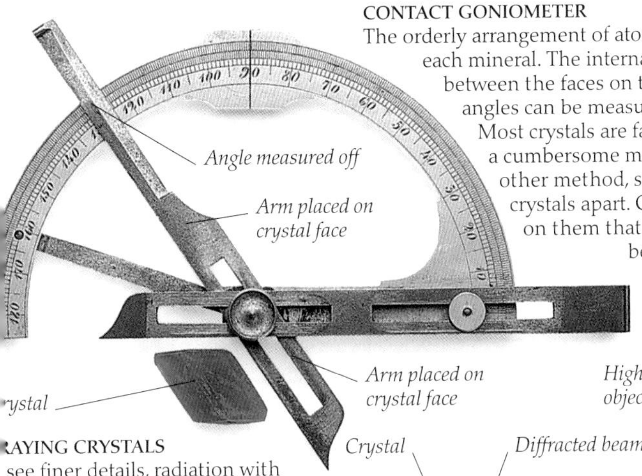
Angle measured off
Arm placed on crystal face
Arm placed on crystal face
›ystal

›AYING CRYSTALS

see finer details, radiation with ›avelength shorter than light is ›eded. This may involve using X-rays ›ere the rays have a wavelength ›ilar in size to the spacings between ›e layers of atoms making up a ›stal. The spacings diffract the X-ray ›am to many different angles. In ›tain directions, the scattered ›ams are in phase and ›nforce one another ›d so make a black point photographic film. ›e result is a unique ›fraction pattern for ›ch mineral relating its internal spacings.

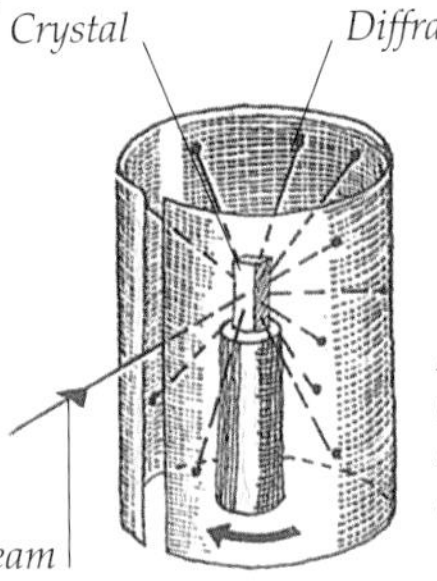
Crystal
Diffracted beams
X-ray beam

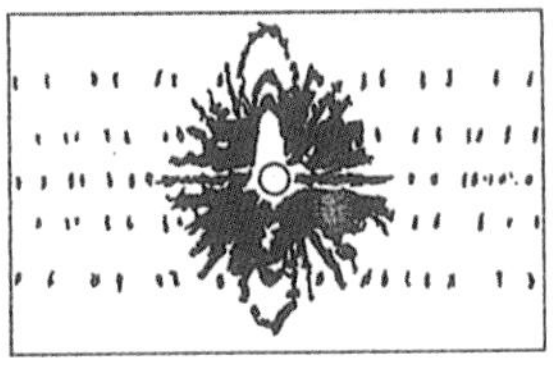
X-ray photograph

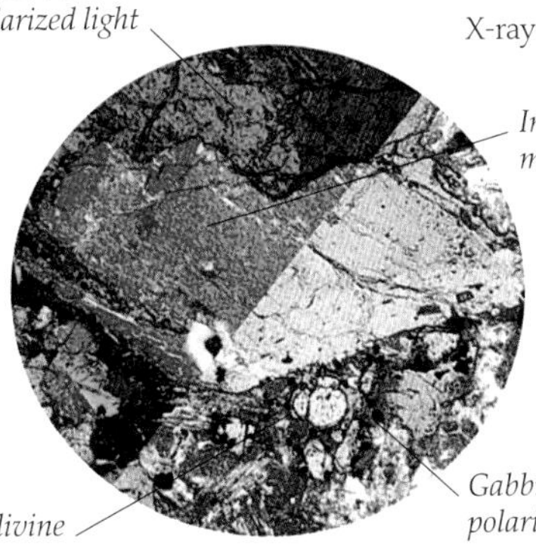
›bbro in cross-›larized light
Interference colors of mineral grains
›livine
Gabbro in plane-polarized light

›ING POLARIZERS

›trologists look at thin sections of rock using polarized ›ht to see the colors, textures, and interrelationships of ›inerals. From this information, they can identify the rock. ›lding a second, crossed polarizer shows interference colors ›at aid further in the identification.

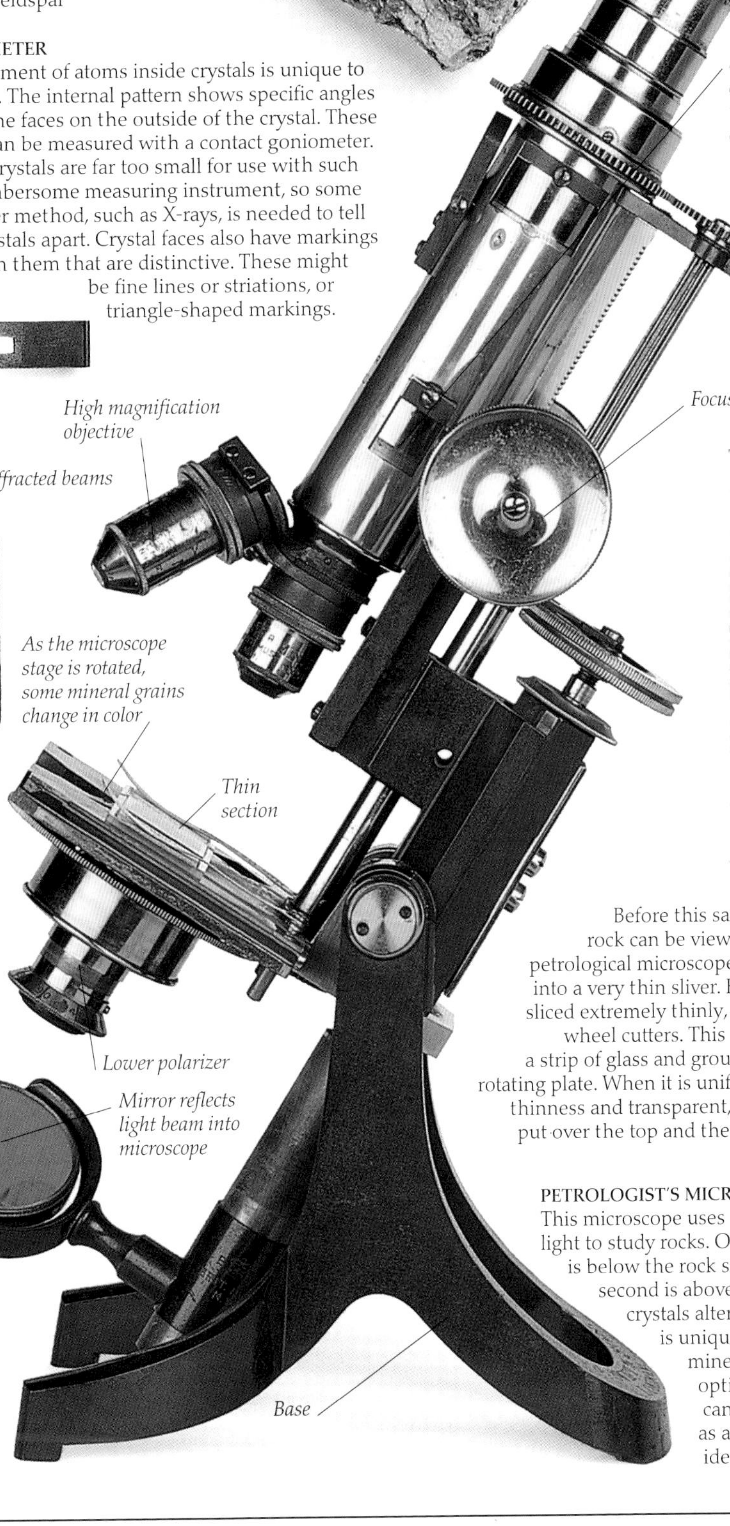
Eyepiece
Second polarizer at a right angle to the first cuts off all light if there is no rock in between
High magnification objective
Focusing knob
As the microscope stage is rotated, some mineral grains change in color
Thin section
Lower polarizer
Mirror reflects light beam into microscope
Base

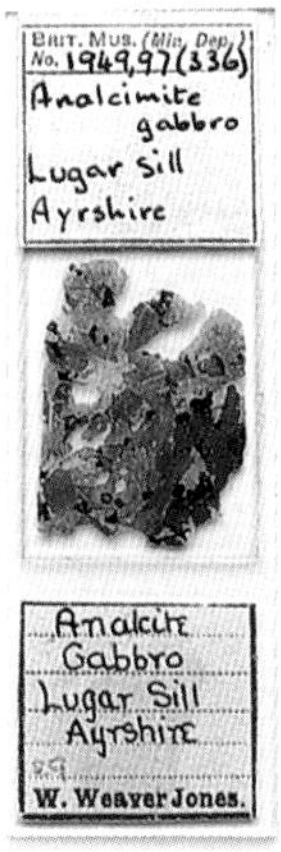
BRIT. MUS. (Min. Dep.) No. 1949,97(336)
Analcimite gabbro
Lugar Sill
Ayrshire
Analcite
Gabbro
Lugar Sill
Ayrshire
W. Weaver Jones.

THIN SECTION

Before this sample of gabbro rock can be viewed through the petrological microscope, it must be cut into a very thin sliver. First, the rock is sliced extremely thinly, using diamond wheel cutters. This slice is glued to a strip of glass and ground further on a rotating plate. When it is uniformly the right thinness and transparent, a glass cover is put over the top and the slice is labeled.

PETROLOGIST'S MICROSCOPE

This microscope uses polarized light to study rocks. One polarizer is below the rock slice, the second is above. The way crystals alter the light is unique to each mineral type, so optical properties can be used as a means of identification.

Igneous rocks

Guy Tancrède de Dolomieu (1750–1801)

Igneous rocks are the primary, original material that makes up the Earth's surface. The first rocks on the Earth were igneous rocks; they formed as the planet started to cool. Magma is the molten material found in the Earth's crust that solidifies and crystallizes in a complex way to make the range of different minerals found in igneous rocks. This process cannot be observed, so scientists must guess at the mechanism. But some magma does reach the surface when it erupts from volcanoes as lava. Because Vesuvius erupted several times in the 18th century, French mineralogist Dolomieu was able to study an active volcano. He became convinced that the origin of the lava was deep inside the Earth. Some magma cools and solidifies inside the Earth's crust in a mass known as an igneous intrusion. At the beginning of the 20th century, Norman Bowen (1887–1956), a Canadian petrologist, studied the way silicate liquids crystallized as they cooled, working with silicate melts which were an approximation to natural magma. He discovered that metal oxide minerals crystallized out first, as they had the highest melting points. The later crystals that formed were a product of interaction between the early crystals and the liquid that remained, which had a different chemical composition.

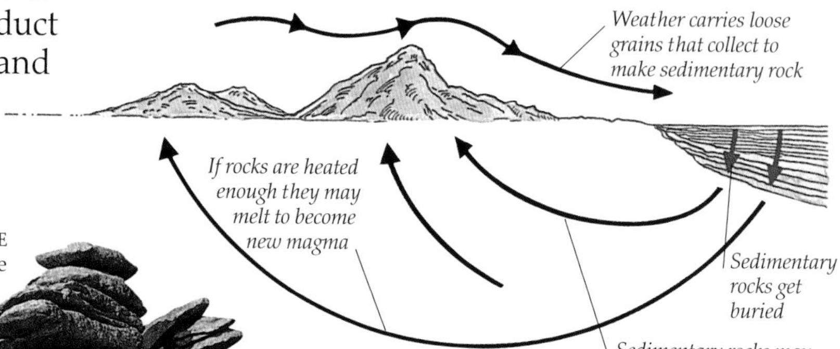

Weather carries loose grains that collect to make sedimentary rock
If rocks are heated enough they may melt to become new magma
Sedimentary rocks get buried
Sedimentary rocks may be heated and compressed into metamorphic rocks

THE ROCK CYCLE

The rock cycle continually renews the surface of the Earth. When igneous rocks meet the Earth's atmosphere, they are changed. New minerals are formed, and the crystal grains are separated and carried away by erosive agents to form sediments. They become sedimentary rock (pp. 26–27) and can then be heated or compressed into metamorphic rock (pp. 28–29), and even melted to make new igneous rock.

WEARING DOWN A MOUNTAIN RANGE

When a mountain range is made, the underlying rocks are elevated (pp. 46–47). As the mountain range grows higher, the mountaintops are worn away by the weather over millions of years. This granite at Dartmoor in England crystallized many miles down in the Earth's crust and was part of an igneous intrusion known as a batholith (p. 51). Erosion has worn away a whole mountain range, leaving the hilltop granite tor, which comes from the Celtic name for granite summits in this part of the world.

Eroded granite

Haytor, Dartmoor, England

Orthorhombic crystals

Monoclinic crystals

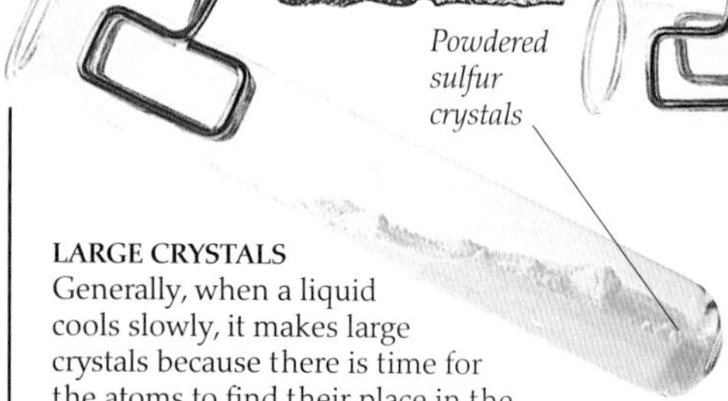

Powdered sulfur crystals

Melted sulfur

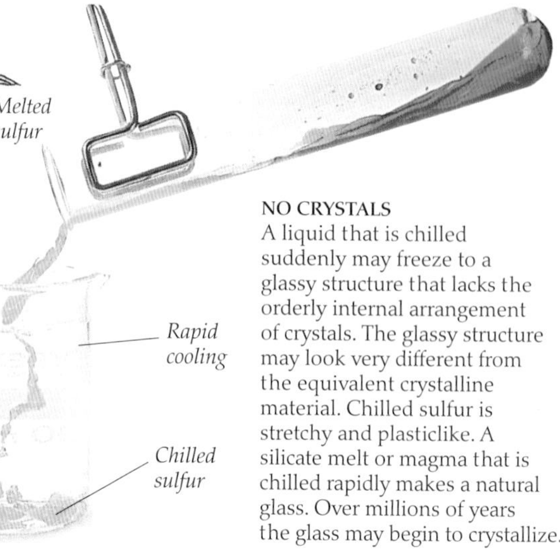

Rapid cooling

Chilled sulfur

LARGE CRYSTALS

Generally, when a liquid cools slowly, it makes large crystals because there is time for the atoms to find their place in the orderly crystal arrangement. The element sulfur makes orthorhombic or monoclinic crystals, depending on the temperature at which the crystals grow. The granite of Haytor cooled over perhaps 1 million years, so the crystals are as large as 2 in (5 cm) across.

SMALL CRYSTALS

Powdered crystals of sulfur can be heated until they melt. If the conditions of cooling are faster, needlelike monoclinic crystals form at about 194°F (90°C). These crystals grow in nature in the heat of a volcanic fumarole, or hot spring. They form around the mouth of the fumarole where the cooling occurs.

NO CRYSTALS

A liquid that is chilled suddenly may freeze to a glassy structure that lacks the orderly internal arrangement of crystals. The glassy structure may look very different from the equivalent crystalline material. Chilled sulfur is stretchy and plasticlike. A silicate melt or magma that is chilled rapidly makes a natural glass. Over millions of years the glass may begin to crystallize.

THE RECYCLING OF MAGMA

Magma originates in the Earth's mantle. Sometimes a little melting takes place in the mantle and if the drops of melt join up they start to migrate toward the Earth's surface. Basalt is the igneous rock nearest in composition to its parent material, the mantle. Basaltlike rocks erupt as lava flows (like those on Hawaii, left) to make up the ocean floor. When the ocean floor goes back into the mantle, part of the basaltic rock is melted. This new magma makes its way back toward the Earth's surface, changing in composition as it travels to become granite.

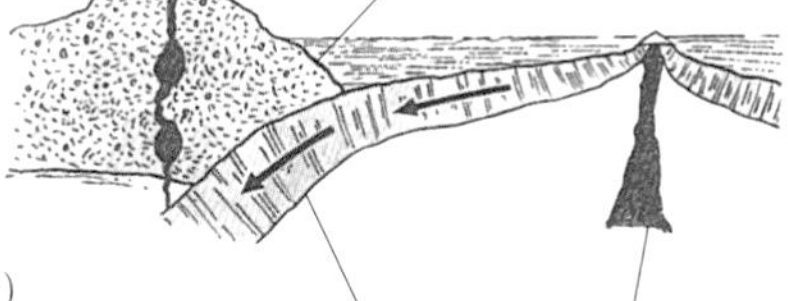
Volcano
Continental crust
Ocean floor slides back into mantle
Rising magma

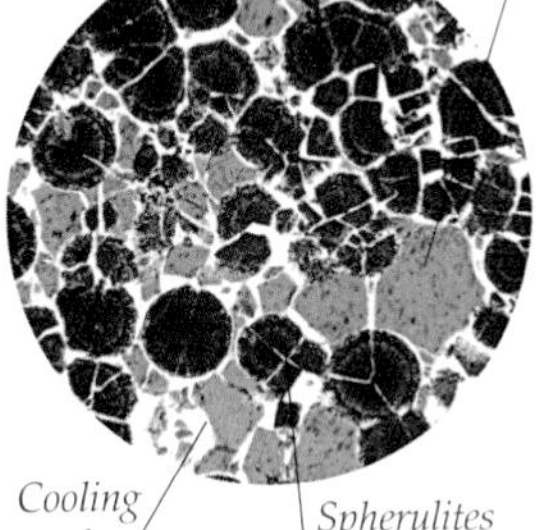
Glass
Cooling cracks
Spherulites are beginnings of crystals

Thin section of obsidian under cross-polarized light

OBSIDIAN

Obsidian is a natural glass made from magma that erupted as lava and cooled too quickly to crystallize. Such fast cooling gives no opportunity for the atoms to arrange themselves in an orderly fashion.

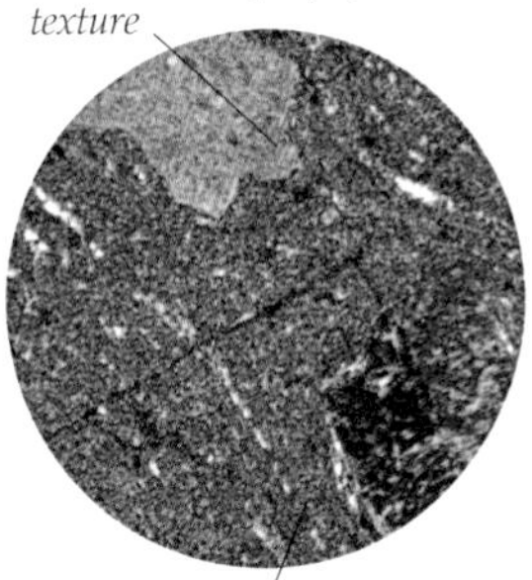
Large crystals against a fine-grained background mass is called porphyritic texture
Crystal cooled as lava flows

Thin section of felsite under cross-polarized light

FELSITE

Felsite's larger crystals of quartz and feldspar grew during slow cooling (before eruption), while the small crystals result from rapid cooling at eruption.

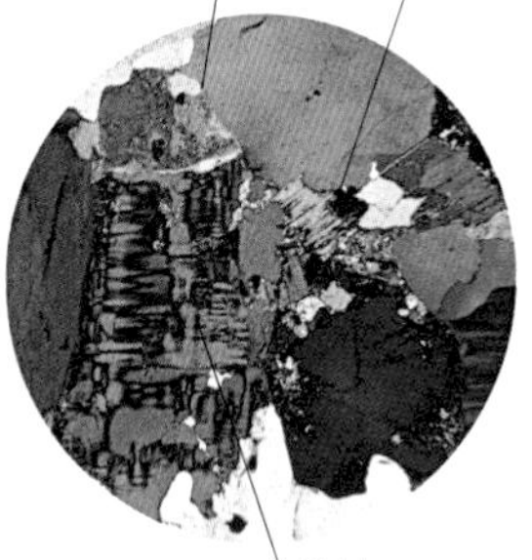
Quartz formed later
Mica fits into spaces
Feldspar crystallized first

Thin section of granite under cross-polarized light

GRANITE

Granite cools most slowly of these three rocks. Obsidian, felsite, and granite are formed from magma of about the same chemical composition—the difference depends on the rate at which they cooled.

Sedimentary rocks

QUARRY OF SAND
The layers of sand in this English quarry are around 100 million years old and were laid in a shallow sea just below the wave depth. The layers of sandstone are overlaid by a layer of gray-colored boulder clay (p. 59). The sand is quarried as sports turf sand for golf courses and fields, and for filtering drinking water.

ROCKS THAT COME INTO CONTACT with the atmosphere and with water are gradually weathered (pp. 50–51), even the hard lavas and granite. Water seeps in between the mineral grains and chemically reacts with the rock to break it down. Particles of the weathered rock are removed by falling rain, or are blown away by the wind and dropped elsewhere. In the new location, layers of sediment are formed, which may become buried by more and more layers. These layers may also contain organic material such as plants and the remains of dead creatures. Eventually the sediments harden and become compacted. Ground water percolates through the sediment, leaving behind minerals that cement the sediment grains together. In this way the sediment is lithified (becomes rock). By understanding how modern sediment forms, it is possible to reconstruct the environment of times gone by—the paleoenvironment—and to make paleogeographic maps showing the geography of land masses that existed many millions of years ago.

WILLIAM SMITH (1769–1839)
Smith was an English engineer who surveyed routes for canals. He recognized the same types of rock in different places and realized that individual layers of sedimentary rock were characterized by similar groupin[gs] of fossils. He concluded that the olde[st] rocks were in the lowest layer.

SANDSTONE
This sandstone is made from grains of sand, like modern desert sand (p. 55). The grains are visible even without a magnifying glass. A specimen of sandstone may also show changes of color and banding. The layers of the original sands may be the result of the desert wind sorting the sand grains into different sizes or densities. Some sandstones show mineral grains in colored bands. These minerals, heavier than ordinary sand grains, are sometimes concentrated in layers.

Grain of quartz

Thin section of sandstone in cross-polarized light

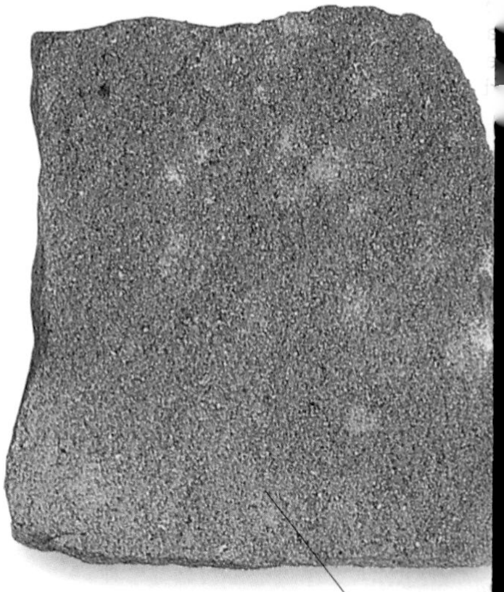

Red sandstone

Even texture

HOW SEDIMENT IS MADE
Fragments of older rocks make up sediment. During a flood, heavy rain loosens the weathered sand and gravel from mountain slopes. Along with the soil (pp. 52–53), this loosened sediment is carried away in flood waters and is dropped when and where the water current slows. A river in flood always has colored turbid water from the sediment it carries, which can be a mixture of mud, sand, and pebbles (p. 57).

Pebble

Origins of oil

Oil is derived from the remains of dead marine plankton. They sink to the seabed, where they become entombed in the thickening sediment. The temperature increases as the sediments are buried ever deeper, and oily liquids are boiled off from the organic remains. The oily material travels through the pores of permeable rocks (p. 15) and seeps into sandstone or limestone. Here, the oil collects in the pore spaces in the rock.

Fossil shell

Shelly limestone

ESTONE
ts and animals live in sea- ver water use um bicarbonate in tion in the water to e calcium carbonate. nals may use this nstruct shells or etons, while plants me surrounded with mud. Eventually the becomes limestone, h often contains the s of the creatures made calcium onate.

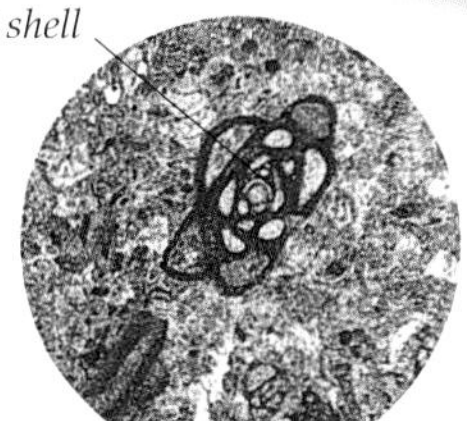
Fossil shell

Thin section of limestone in plane-polarized light

MUDSTONE
It is impossible to see the grains that make up mudstone without a high-powered microscope. The minute flakes of clay and silt are the smallest particles of sediment to come from the weathering of older rocks. Clay is derived from weathering of feldspars. Grains of silt, which might be quartz or feldspar, are slightly larger in size. Mudstone forms in river estuaries, lakes, and in the ocean.

les are
of the
mineral quartz

CONGLOMERATE
Sediment that contains many rounded pebbles, usually with some sand filling in the spaces between, is called conglomerate. Originally the sediment may have been gravel in a riverbed, the pebbles having been carried along during a flood and dumped along with sand.

Sandstone borehole core

Natural oil

OIL-BEARING ROCK
When sediment becomes rock, there are almost always spaces between the individual grains of sediment that are not filled with cementing minerals. In the pore spaces of this sandstone rock, 3 pints (1.5 liters) of oil were trapped under pressure. However, it is not possible to extract all oil from rock. Because of the surface tension and the viscosity of oil, some oil continues to cling to the rock grains.

DRILLING FOR OIL
If a rock structure is suitable, oil sometimes collects. If it is trapped in the rock layers, it can be collected for commercial use. Potential oil-bearing structures may be detected from the Earth's surface or the seabed. The geologist plays a vital role in predicting where oil traps might exist.

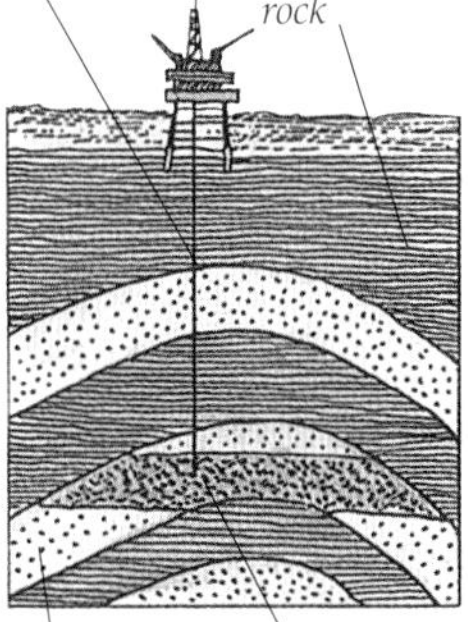
Pipeline
Drilling rig
Impermeable rock
Permeable rock
Trapped oil

Shell
Sand

Metamorphic rocks

THE EXPERIMENTER
Sir James Hall (1761–1832) was a Scottish baronet who took powdered limestone and sealed it in a gun barrel to maintain the pressure, then heated it in his foundry. The material that emerged was a crystalline marble. He had metamorphosed the sedimentary rock.

METAMORPHIC ROCKS ARE ROCKS that have been changed. Previously, they were igneous, sedimentary, or other metamorphic rocks. Almost all metamorphism happens deep in young mountain ranges, as rocks are folded and compressed underneath other rocks. Although the rock never actually melts, its texture and nature may become "like new," made of different, metamorphic crystals (p. 23), with no sign of the original minerals or textures. Part of this occurs in response to pressure, and part is the result of the heat. Metamorphism takes a long time, first for the rock to be buried to a depth where metamorphism can begin, and then for the solid recrystallization to take place. Eventually, metamorphic rocks are exposed at the Earth's surface, but only after the mountain chain is uplifted and eroded deeply (pp. 46–47). This process in which sediment is buried and made into metamorphic rocks may take millions of years.

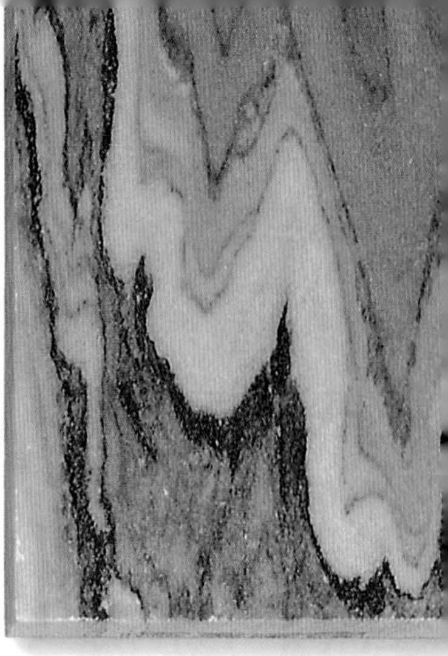

STREAKED CIPOLLINO MARBLE
Limestone made of pure calcium carbonate (p. 27) recrystallizes during metamorphism to a pure white marble. Many limestones contain quartz sand, or some clay, or iron. When these are metamorphosed, the result is colored marble, often with folded banding. Many metamorphic rocks show evidence of folding or fracturing, indicating that they reacted as though they were either plastic or brittle during mountain building.

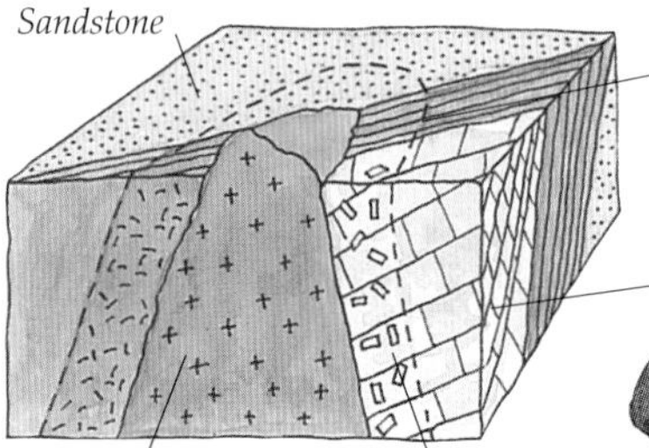
Sandstone
Metamorphic aureole
Limestone
Granite
Marble

CONTACT WITH HOT GRANITE
When molten granite intrudes into rocks in mountain ranges, the rocks are metamorphosed around the granite. The halo of changed rock is called a metamorphic aureole. New minerals grow in response to high temperatures, for example, limestone becomes marble.

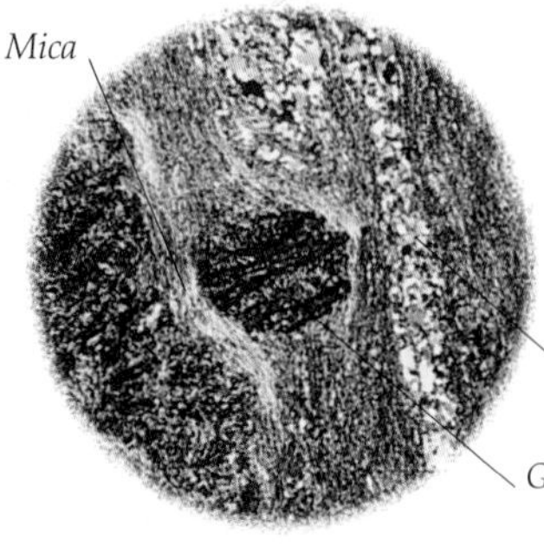
Mica
Quartz
Garnet

MUDSTONE MAKES GARNET
In mudstone, the first metamorphic minerals to grow are mica crystals, orientating themselves in the direction of least pressure. The garnet grew later, pushing mica crystals out of the way.

INCREASING THE PRESSURE
Metamorphism can transform a featureless mudstone into a sparkling crystalline rock. Muds laid down in shallow seas are carried down during mountain building to deeper levels. The first sign of metamorphism is growth of microscopic crystals of mica. Pressure may cause these to be aligned, which produces slate (1). Phyllite (2) has been recrystallized more intensely, so that the mica crystals are larger and can be seen as a shimmer on the rock surface. Even deeper or longer burial in the mountain range creates a schist which may have large mica crystals, and grains or crystals of kyanite (3), whose crystallization is also helped by heat.

SPLITTING SLATE FOR ROOFS
Mica crystals in slate are all parallel to each other. The slate splitter knows the direction, and splits, or cleaves, the slate along it. This is called the cleavage direction.

Increase in pressure

1. Slate

2. Phyllite

Blue kyanite

3. Kyanite schist

Chiastolite
crystal
1. Chiastolite hornfels

Garnet
2. Garnet hornfels

Increase in heat and pressure

Mica-rich
area
Quartz-
rich area
3. Migmatite

AT AND PRESSURE

dstone or shale can grow crystals of the mineral astolite (1) when it is in contact with magma. resulting hard rock is called hornfels. More nse metamorphism, at greater depth and perature, may grow garnet crystals (2) instead. nse metamorphism, where rock is heated almost nelting, produces migmatite, or mixed rock (3).

Mica-rich
layers weather
more easily

IONAL METAMORPHISM

s gneiss in northern France was part of a mountain range t was eroded down to a plain long before the Alps were ned. Gneiss is a rock formed through metamorphism of ole regions. Such regional metamorphism happens during birth of a mountain range.

SOLID-STATE RECRYSTALLIZATION

All the recrystallization that is part of metamorphism happens in the solid state. It is similar to the recrystallization that happens when metal is heated and beaten to make wrought iron. The original metal is made of crystals which, after heating in the furnace, adjust their structure in response to the pressure applied by beating. At the points where crystals meet, individual atoms move away to a place where pressure is lower. There they align themselves with the crystal structure and add on to it.

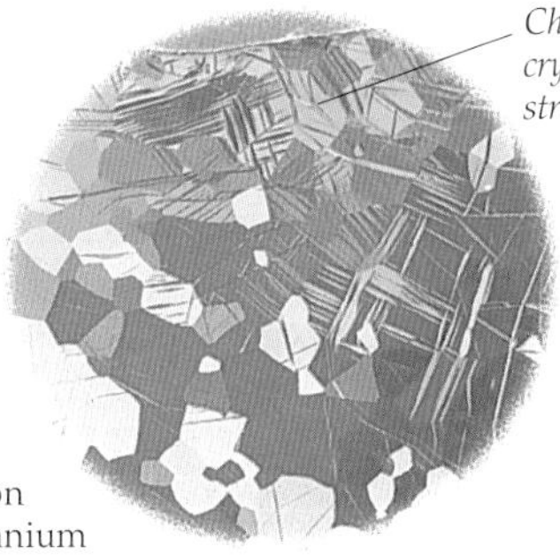
Changed
crystal
structure
Thin section of titanium

ROLLED METAL

The texture of this titanium metal has been altered by cold rolling. Crystals near the surface have responded to the pressure put on them and have adjusted their structure to fit in with it. In the same way, but with heating as well, rocks metamorphose without melting. Under some circumstances, melting may take place in mountain ranges, making a new magma. This can happen if very hot granite magmas ascend in an active mountain range and cause melting of the surrounding rocks, increasing the volume of the granite magma.

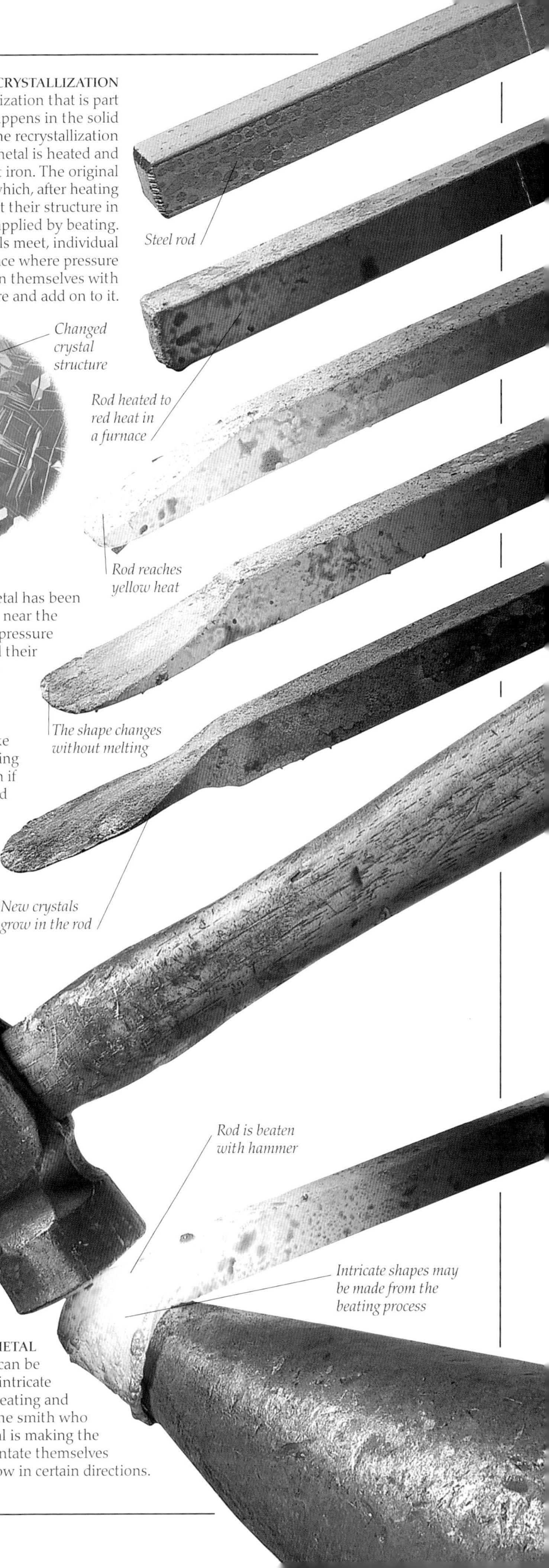
Steel rod
Rod heated to
red heat in
a furnace
Rod reaches
yellow heat
The shape changes
without melting
New crystals
grow in the rod
Rod is beaten
with hammer
Intricate shapes may
be made from the
beating process

RED-HOT METAL

A plain steel rod can be fashioned into intricate patterns by heating and beating it. The smith who works the metal is making the crystals reorientate themselves as they grow in certain directions.

The challenge of the ocean

THE BEGINNINGS OF MODERN OCEANOGRAPHY lie at the end of the 19th century, with oceanic surveys such as those conducted by the British research vessel *Challenger*. The US was proposing to explore the Atlantic and Pacific oceans, with Alexandre Agassiz (1835–1910) as joint leader, and German and Swedish ships, too, were venturing into the Atlantic. The British government was persuaded to support the *Challenger* expedition to uphold Britain's international prestige. It was hoped that *Challenger*'s exploration would be able to answer pressing questions of the day. Was the deep ocean populated with living creatures? Could ocean currents be measured to confirm theories about how oceanic waters circulated? If sediment lay on the ocean floor, would it be the familiar chalk? *Challenger* was able to answer some of these questions, but the oceanic circulation remained a controversy even at the end of the voyage. It is now known that many variable factors influence the currents. By taking depth soundings, *Challenger* did discover submarine mountains in the middle of the Atlantic Ocean (pp. 38–39), and found the Mariana Trench, 36,000 ft (11,033 m) down in the Pacific Ocean.

IMAGINING THE DEEP
In 1869 French writer Jules Verne (1828–1905) wrote the science-fiction novel *Twenty Thousand Leagues under the Sea*. It tells of a submarine whose technology was advanced far beyond its time. In the 21st century the technology of Verne's submarine is commonplace, but Verne was writing at a time when the undersea world was unexplored.

END OF THE FLAT-EARTH THEORY
In the 16th century, an expedition led by the Portuguese explorer Ferdinand Magellan (1480–1521) sailed around the world, finally proving that it was not flat. Magellan tried to calculate the depth of the ocean as he sailed. Navigators, however, usually kept in sight of land. Here, the water is shallower than in the great ocean depths, and the bottom sediments are derived from the land.

Glass flask

Mercury acts as a weight

THE HYDROMETER
Oceanic water was sampled by *Challenger* to discover how salinity and temperature vary with depth and location. This hydrometer measured salinity. The warm surface current in the Atlantic Ocean—the Gulf Stream—was already known, mapped by Benjamin Franklin in the 18th century. *Challenger* showed that there was much colder water at deeper levels that could be the compensating current of cold water.

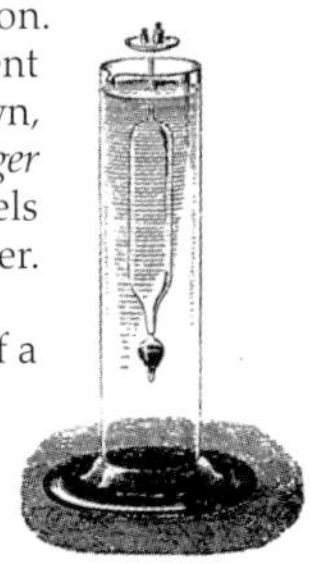

Engraving of a hydrometer suspended in liquid

HISTORIC VOYAGE
The *Challenger*'s epic voyage lasted from 1872 to 1876. The ship sailed 68,890 nautical miles (79,277 miles/ 127,584 km), measuring the ocean and collecting samples. The expedition did not include a physicist. If it had, perhaps the profusion of *Challenger*'s observations could have been used to determine the interrelationships between salinity, temperature and water density, ocean bottom slope, winds, and the effects of evaporation and rainfall, which together affect oceanic circulation.

ng through dredged sediment on *Challenger*

ON BOARD SHIP
The naturalists on *Challenger* charted ocean-bottom sediments and their relationship to life in the sea. Dredges were used to sample these sediments. The samples showed that the plankton *Globigerina* lived in the surface water of almost all parts of the ocean. Investigations showed that when *Globigerina* dies, the shells sink to the seabed and make the fine carbonate mud known as Globigerina ooze (p. 13).

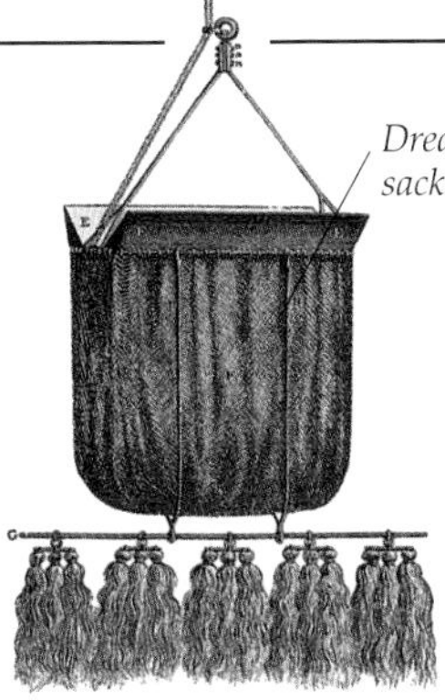

Dredge sack
Flat-headed swabs drag the net along the seafloor

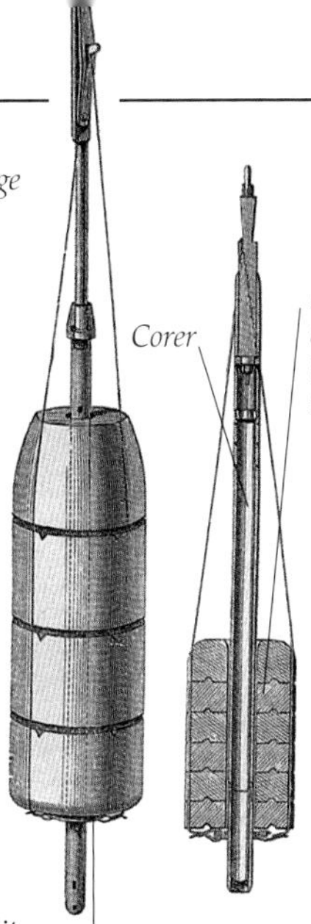

Corer
Iron sinkers detach before resurfacing
Iron sinkers carry line down and force the corer into the sludge

DREDGING THE DEPTHS
Dredges and cores (p. 13) were used to collect material from all parts of the seabed. Although water samples showed that *Globigerina* lived in the sunlit shallow waters of the Atlantic, the dredges brought up reddish-colored clay from the deep ocean floor instead of the ooze. The deeper the water, the less sign there was of any *Globigerina* shells at the ocean bed. The *Challenger* team supposed, rightly, that at such huge depths *Globigerina* shells had dissolved in seawater; the red clay was dust blown from the land.

Slides containing samples

Clay from seashore | Globigerina ooze | Shelly sand | Sediment

ASSEMBLING THE EVIDENCE
The task of sending samples to scientists for study and storage and of writing up and publishing the results of *Challenger*'s work took 15 years. The material was bottled with labels that gave latitude and longitude, the depth of water where the sample was collected, and the type of material (ooze or clay, for example).

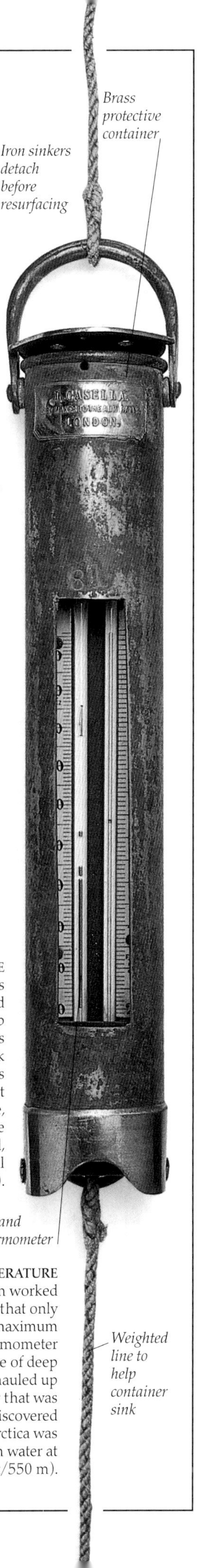

Brass protective container
J. CASELLA
LONDON
Mercury and glass thermometer
Weighted line to help container sink

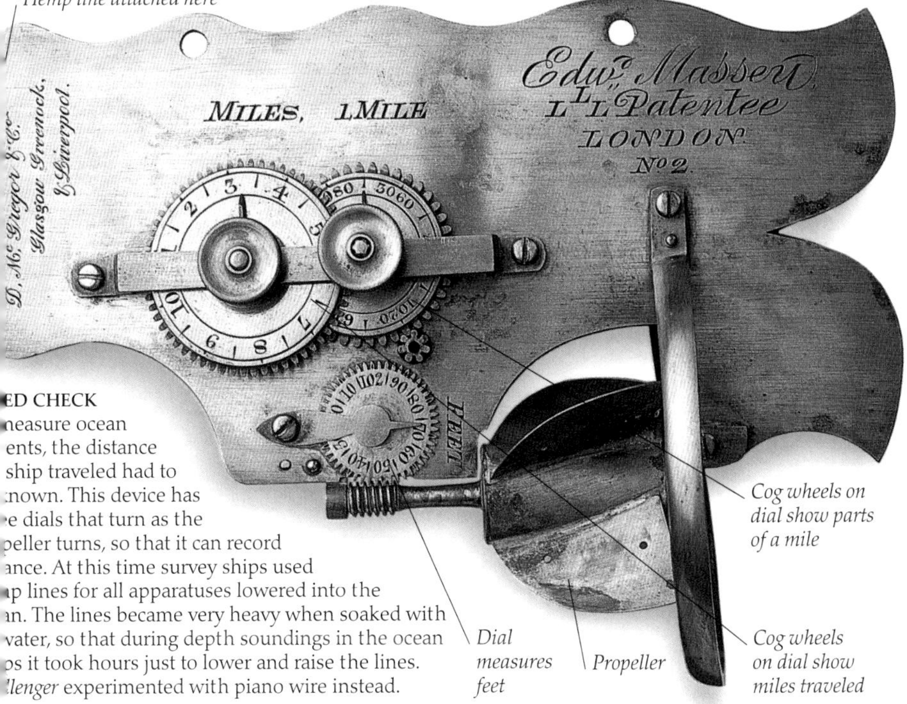

Hemp line attached here
MILES, 1 MILE
Edwd. Massey
L. L. Patentee
LONDON
No 2
D. McGregor & Co. Glasgow Greenock & Liverpool.
FEET
Cog wheels on dial show parts of a mile
Dial measures feet
Propeller
Cog wheels on dial show miles traveled

ED CHECK
neasure ocean ents, the distance ship traveled had to nown. This device has e dials that turn as the peller turns, so that it can record ance. At this time survey ships used p lines for all apparatuses lowered into the n. The lines became very heavy when soaked with vater, so that during depth soundings in the ocean os it took hours just to lower and raise the lines. *llenger* experimented with piano wire instead.

TAKING THE TEMPERATURE
At first, the *Challenger* team worked with thermometers that only recorded minimum and maximum temperatures. The thermometer registered the temperature of deep water even when it was hauled up to the ship through water that was cooler or warmer. It was discovered that surface water off Antarctica was 3°F (1.67°C) colder than water at 300 fathoms (1,800 ft/550 m).

Modern oceanography

LIFE IN THE OCEAN DEPTHS
The deep ocean is a dark place. Knowing the amount of light in ocean water is vital to our understanding of where and how oceanic plants and animals live. Photosynthesis can take place at light levels as low as 1 percent of sunlight. Creatures like the angler fish, which emit light to lure their prey, add significantly to light levels in the dark parts of the ocean.

TWENTIETH-CENTURY OCEANOGRAPHIC SURVEYS have revolutioniz our view of the planet and how it works by revealing the surface features—the topography—and nature of the ocean floor. In the earl 1960s, a plan took shape to drill a borehole into the mantle. The "Mohole" was to be drilled where the crust was thinnest. This involvec drilling in deep water from a floating ship. Seismic investigation (p. 40 had already shown that the ocean floor has a layered structure. The Mohole would sample the ocean floor and reveal the nature of the layers. Mohole never reached the Moho—the boundary where the mantle meets the crust (p. 40). Instead, in 1968, the US drilling ship *Glomar Challenger* began to roam the oceans, drilling into sediment and the ocean floor. Detailed mapping is now carried out by remote sensing apparatuses towed from floating ships and housed in orbiting satellites. Computers are used to visualize oceanic water circulation.

INVESTIGATING THE
Glomar Challenger's samples led understanding of seafloor sprea (pp. 38–39). They revealed that neare the submarine mountains (p. 30) the b is young, and farther away it is older only that, but near these ridges the o sediments on the hard basaltic floo present-day sediments. Farther fron ridge, these present-day sedimen over progressively older sedim

PLANKTON NETS
The food chain in the oceans begins with the inorganic nutrients carried in oceanic currents. The smallest algae and animals are plankton, which float passively. They range from microscopic algae to shrimp. The larger ocean life feeds on this plankton. Oceanographers use special plankton nets to assess the amounts of plankton, and to discover the relative proportions of algal and animal plankton in a given area. Sampling in the seas around Antarctica showed that in oceanic water the animal plankton grazed on the algal plankton, but in coastal waters they fed on bacteria.

PLANKTON FROM SATELLITE
Modern oceanographers and marine geologists use sophisticated technology in their work. Satellites can map the distribution of plankton in surface water—here in the Indian and Pacific oceans. Satellite imagery can also help to spot changes in temperature and salinity in oceanic waters, which, though small, may have profound effects on oceanic currents.

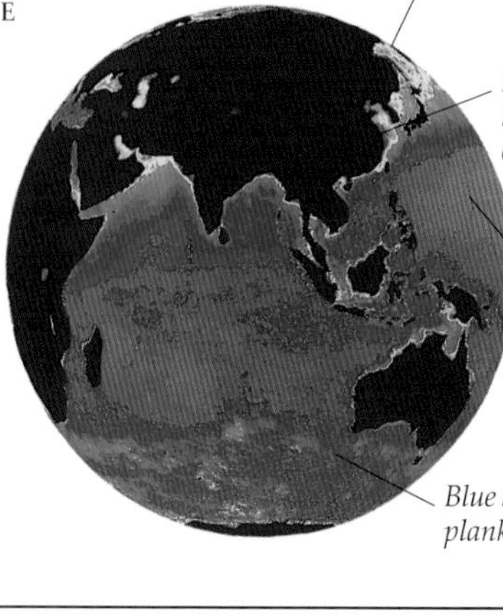

Yellow shows average plankton density

Red shows the highest density of plankton

Pink shows the lowest density of plankton

Blue shows a low plankton density

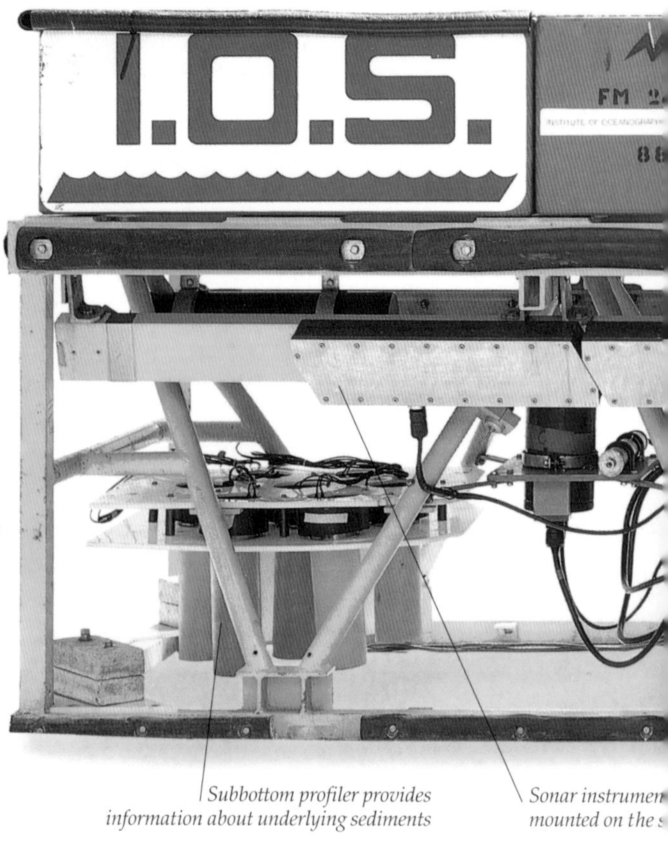

Subbottom profiler provides information about underlying sediments

Sonar instrumen mounted on the s

›nar imaging

›cean water, below a few hundred ›ds, it is too dark for light imaging to us anything about the ocean floor. ›ınd waves, however, can be used ›tead. Echo sounding was the first ›h method. Modern sophisticated ›ınd imaging with computer ›ancement can now ›e detailed pictures, and ›ke maps of areas of ›cial interest, such as ›economic exclusion ›ıes off coastlines.

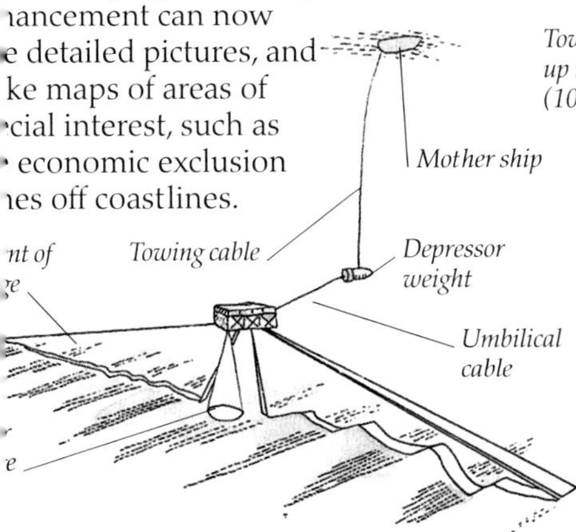

Mother ship
Towing cable
Depressor weight
Umbilical cable

›W SONAR WORKS
›ustic images of the ocean floor can be produced by a scanner that ›smits regular sound pulses. The echoes show up on a display. ›units which make up the image (pixels) cover an area the size of ›ol table. Future developments may include a scatterometer to ›rmine the character of the sediment while fiber-optic towing ›es will bring the possibility of remote-videoing.

›VED OCEAN BOTTOM INSTRUMENT (TOBI)
›BI is a remote-controlled vehicle that is towed behind a ship ›ater up to 20,000 ft (6000 m) deep. It acts as a platform for ›riety of oceanographic instruments. Its sensors send data ›ugh the umbilical cable to the ship, where they are stored ›n optical disk. The sound pictures, called sonographs, can ›ge by sonar an object as small as 6 ft (2 m) across.

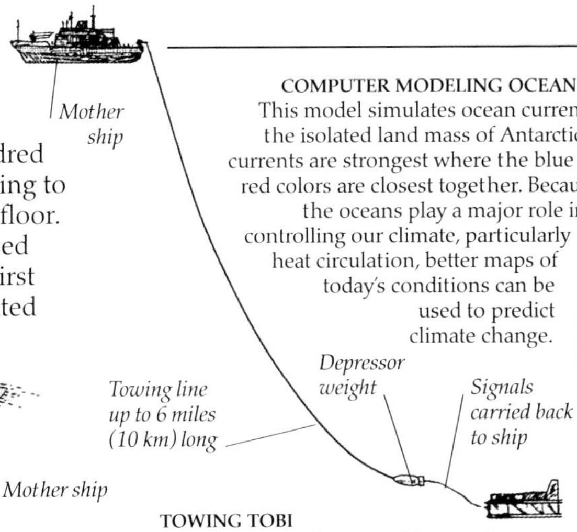

Mother ship
Towing line up to 6 miles (10 km) long
Depressor weight
Signals carried back to ship

TOWING TOBI
TOBI (see below) is towed from a ship using a line and weight that allows it to remain horizontal in the sea. TOBI has a range of 2 miles (3 km) and is towed about 1,000 ft (300 m) above the seabed at a speed of 3 knots (3½ mph/5.5 kph).

COMPUTER MODELING OCEAN CURRENTS
This model simulates ocean currents around the isolated land mass of Antarctica. The currents are strongest where the blue and red colors are closest together. Because the oceans play a major role in controlling our climate, particularly heat circulation, better maps of today's conditions can be used to predict climate change.

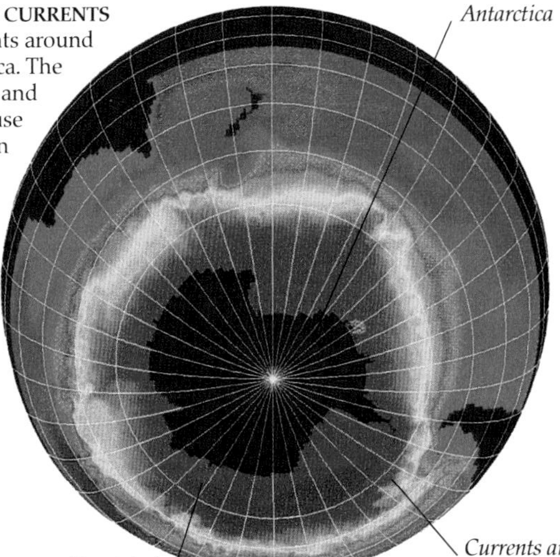

Antarctica
Simulated ocean currents
Currents are strongest where blue and red are close together

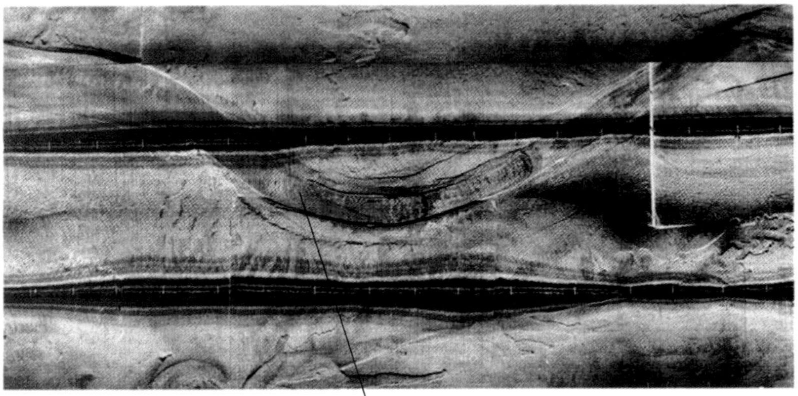

River channel

Submarine river valley off the West Coast of the US

SUBMARINE RIVER
This TOBI image shows a submarine river valley scoured by flowing sediments. The sediment would normally sit on the continental shelf, but it has been disturbed and has flowed down the shelf to the ocean floor.

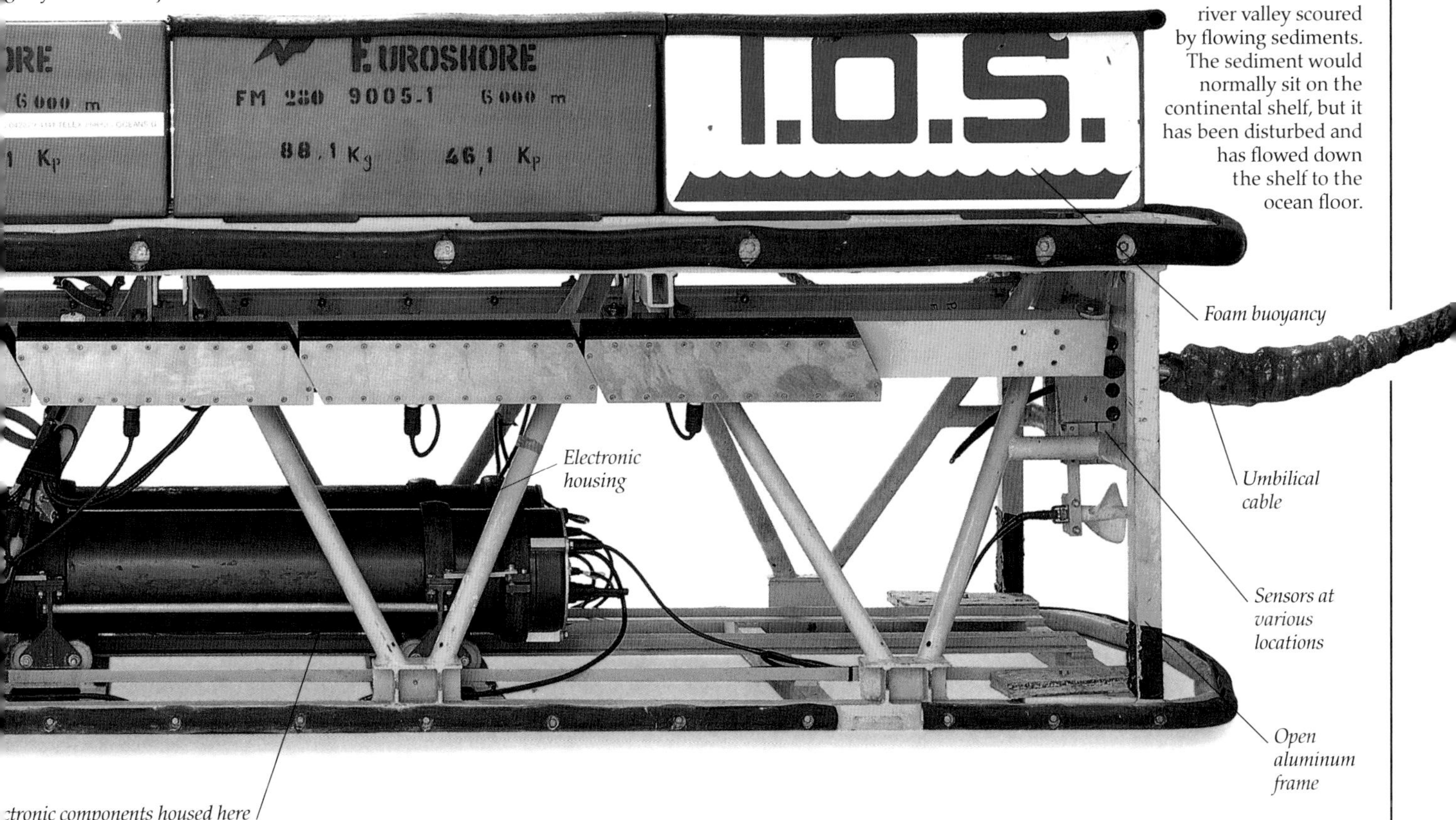

›RE
6 000 m
1 Kp
EUROSHORE
FM 280 9005-1 6 000 m
88,1 Kg 46,1 Kp
I.O.S.
Foam buoyancy
Electronic housing
Umbilical cable
Sensors at various locations
Open aluminum frame
›tronic components housed here

Continental drift

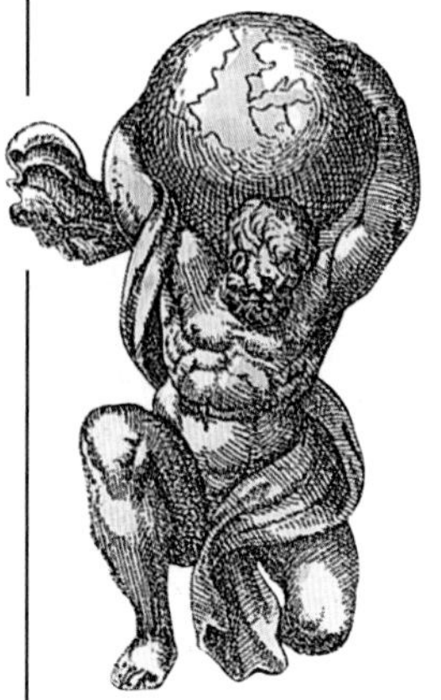

Atlas holding the world on his shoulders

The shapes and sizes of the continents are continually changing, although extremely slowly. The earliest maps of the south Atlantic Ocean showed a remarkable fit between the shapes of the coastlines on each side. It took time to understand what kind of mechanism could move the continents to make this happen (pp. 36–37). It is now known that the continents are moving, and the rate—only an inch or so a year—can be measured. In 1915, Alfred Wegener (1880–1930) published his theory of drifting continents. This told of an ancient "supercontinent" that scientists called Pangaea. When Pangaea started to break up some 300 million years ago (abbreviated to 300 mya), the Atlantic Ocean began to grow in the place where Africa split away from South America. Eduard Suess (p. 42) proposed that the southern continent be called Gondwanaland, after a region inhabited by the Gonds in India. Slightly later, the northern continent Laurasia was split apart to separate North America from Europe, isolating Greenland. It seems that the Earth's processes continually either split supercontinents apart or move continents together to make supercontinents, in cyclic events that take hundreds of millions of years to complete.

SIR FRANCIS BACON (1561–1626)
Following the discovery of America and the mapping of the coastlines of th Atlantic Ocean, the English philosophe Francis Bacon suggested that the coastl of the two continents seemed to fit eac other as though they had been torn apa

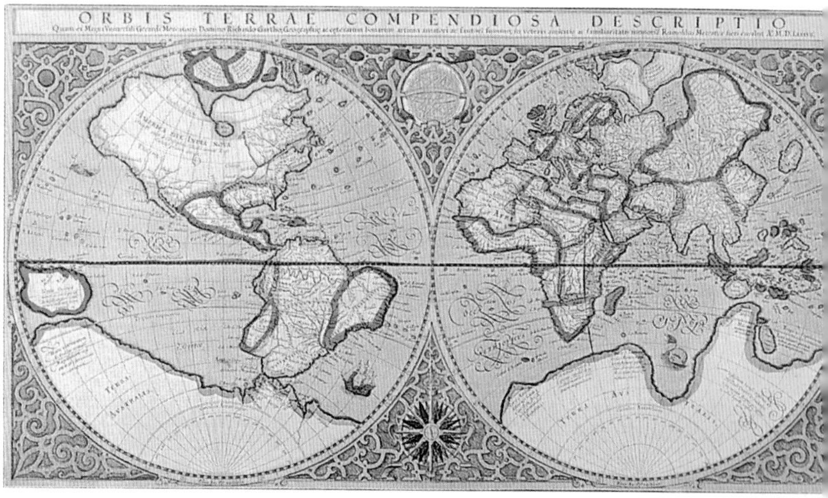

MAPPING THE WORLD
In 1569, Flemish cartographer Gerardus Mercator (1512–94) produced a world map based on knowledge brought back by the navigators of the time. Coastlines were becoming better known from exploration of the Americas and the Pacific Ocean. The journeys of Magellan, Vasco de Gama, and Columbus had, in a short period, doubled the known area of the Earth. Mercator's map showed that the land areas are only a small part of the surface of the Earth, with the ocean regions covering three-quarters of the map. Ancient ideas about the ocean, its depth, and its surface extent were previously vague.

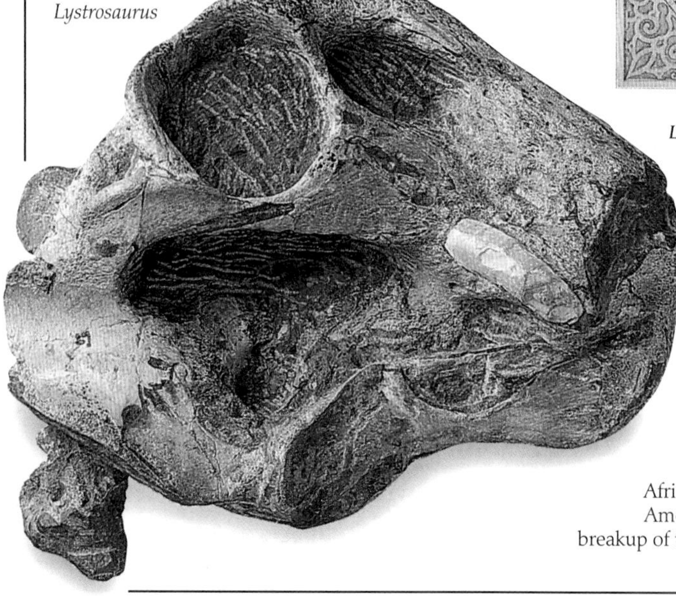

The skull of *Lystrosaurus*

LYSTROSAURUS
Fossil remains of land-dwelling animals such as *Lystrosaurus* show that the southern continents were once linked together. The same types of fossil are found in all the southern continents; the animals must have roamed freely over lands now separated by ocean.

Namibian coastline

NAMIBIAN DESERT
Rocks found in Namibia in western Africa are similar to those in Brazil in South America. They were formed long before the breakup of the southern continent Gondwanaland.

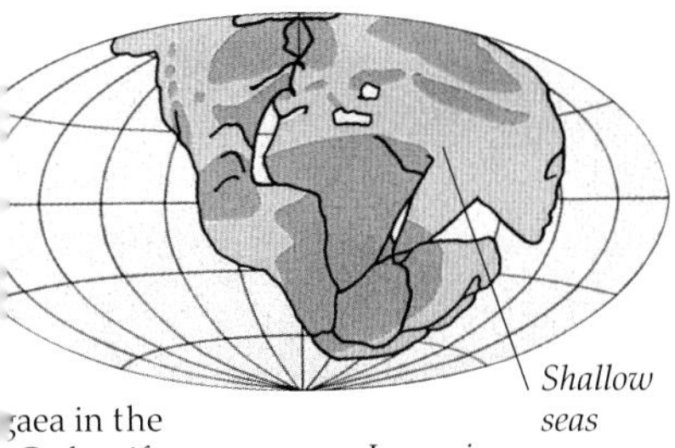
Shallow seas
;aea in the Carboniferous

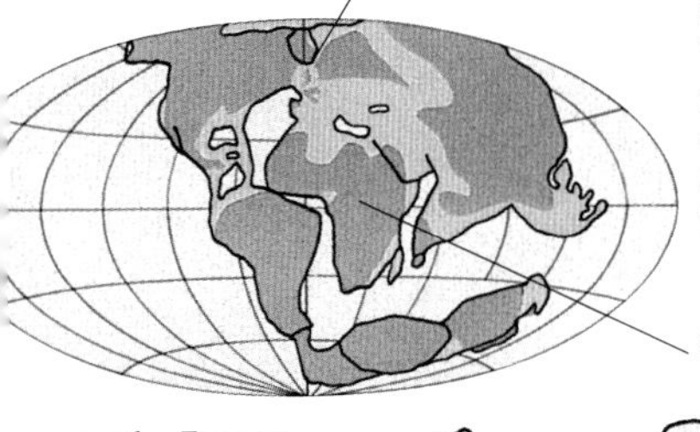
Laurasia
Gondwanaland
;aea in the Eocene

PANGAEA
Wegener's maps of the drifting continents placed them all together in Late Carboniferous times as the great supercontinent that he called Pangaea, a Greek name for "all the Earth." In the Eocene period, Greenland still connected Europe and North America. Geologists were divided in their acceptance of Wegener's elegant idea, mainly because geophysicists could not suggest a mechanism for how the continents moved.

Common snail

SUPPORTING EVIDENCE
Formidable data supported Wegener's theory. The distributions of plants and land animals in North America and western Europe were shown to have many similarities. The garden snail, found in southern Germany and the British Isles, was also found in the eastern US.

Alfred Wegener

GONDWANALAND DRIFTING
Wegener drew the southern continents close to the South Pole because Carboniferous rocks showed that part of Gondwanaland was covered with an ice sheet. Matching lavas 200 million years old are found in both Africa and South America. These eruptions of lava may have been part of the deep rifting that started the breakup of Gondwanaland.

GONDWANALAND
AFRICA
INDIA
AUSTRALIA
ANTARCTICA
SOUTH AMERICA
Arrows show direction of movement
ure split ontinental dmass
Identical fossils have been found in lands far apart
Glaciated area

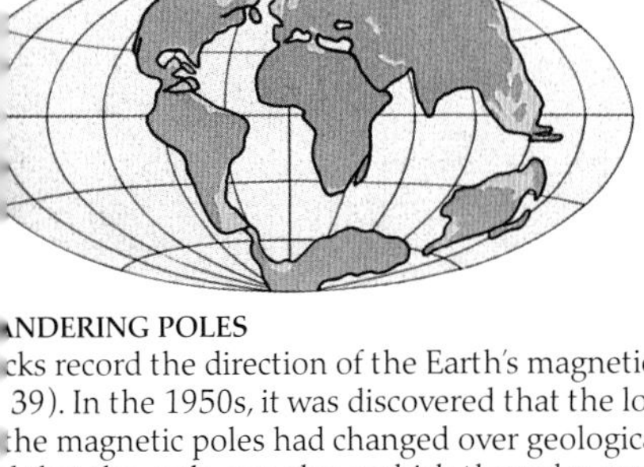
e Tertiary

FAST-MOVING INDIA
While Pangaea was splitting, the movement of India was complex. Its direction and speed of movement has been worked out from the magnetism of lavas that were poured out over millions of years in the Deccan Plateau in India. Analyzing these lavas showed that India's latitude has changed over time. The older lavas showed a location around 60°S. India then moved rapidly north, travelling at 1 in (2.5 cm) per year, until it began to collide with Asia 55 million years ago, at which time Asia extended farther south than today (p. 49). This lost land is now crushed up into the Tibetan Plateau.

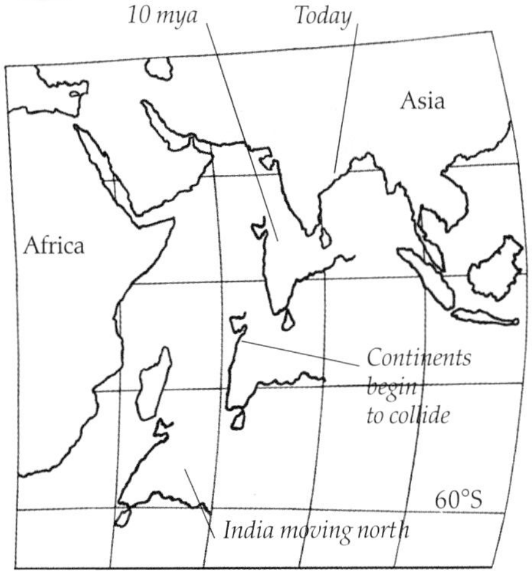
10 mya
Today
Asia
Africa
Continents begin to collide
60°S
India moving north

NDERING POLES
cks record the direction of the Earth's magnetic field 39). In the 1950s, it was discovered that the location he magnetic poles had changed over geological time, l that the pathways along which the poles appeared wander was not the same in individual continents. By 50, however, it was clear that these wandering pathways ıld be superimposed by closing up the Atlantic Ocean, porting Wegener's continental drift hypothesis.

Global relief image of the topography of the South Pole and the Pacific, Indian, and Antarctic oceans

Plate tectonics

FORTY YEARS AFTER ALFRED WEGENER put forward his controversial continental drift theory (pp. 34–35), technological advances revealed a great deal of information about the ocean floor (pp. 38–39). The discovery of magnetic stripes by two British research scientists, F. Vine and D. Matthews, in 1963 and independently by Canadian geologist Lawrence Morley suggested that the ocean floor was made of younger rock than that on the continents. This led to the all-embracing theory of plate tectonics, which divides the world into plates, made up of parts of continent and parts of ocean. For example, the South American plate includes half the south Atlantic Ocean, as well as the continental mass of South America. New plate is being made all the time at spreading ridges (the submarine mountains found by *Challenger*, p. 30) in the oceans, and old oceanic plate material is being recycled in subduction zones. In the process of subduction (p. 43), some oceanic sediments and even whole islands are added to the continents. Plate tectonics also helps to explain the coincidence between lines of volcanoes, deep ocean trenches, and the location of earthquakes.

AN ALTERNATIVE THEORY
In 1931, British geologist Arthur Holmes (1890–1965) came up with the idea for a mechanism that might allow land masses to move. He suggested that hot currents rising under the oceanic ridges and descending at the edges of the continents were responsible for the movements of continents. He had no observations at this time to support his theory. Holmes was also a pioneer of radiometric dating (pp. 60–61).

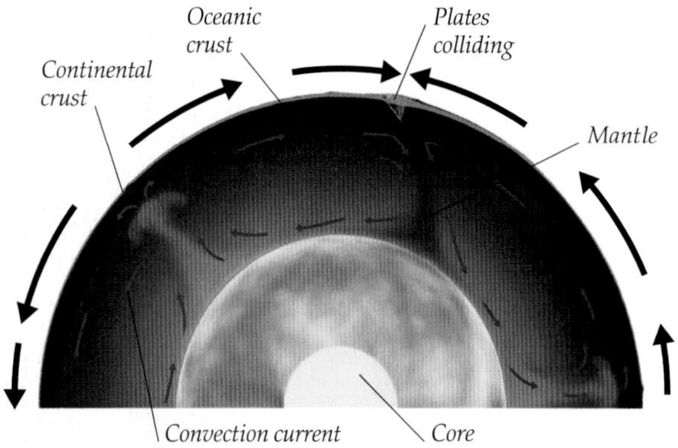
Oceanic crust
Plates colliding
Continental crust
Mantle
Convection current
Core

THE MOVING PLATES
There is still controversy about what moves the plates over the surface of the Earth. Possibly, convection currents in the mantle help to push them. Heat rises and convection occurs as heat is lost from the core to the mantle. The currents move very slowly and carry the plates along. As cooled mantle descends, it is replaced by new hot mantle. Scientists believe that the mantle is unresponsive to short-term events like the sudden shock of earthquake waves passing through. In response to long-term stress applied over tens of millions of years, however, it can move by slow flow. The mantle slowly evolves as it convects, giving up some of its substance to magmas that make up new edges of plate.

PLATE TECTONIC MAP OF THE WORLD
Plate boundaries, or margins, divide up the surface of the Earth. Some pass very close to the junctions between continents and oceans, but the great majority bear no relationship to the edges of the continents. The Australian plate contains Australia and a large part of the Indian Ocean, as well as other surrounding oceans. Today, all oceanic crust is less than 200 million years old. It has solidified from magma over this time at the spreading ridges (pp. 38–39). Any older oceanic crust has been consumed in subduction zones (p. 43). By contrast, the continents are much older.

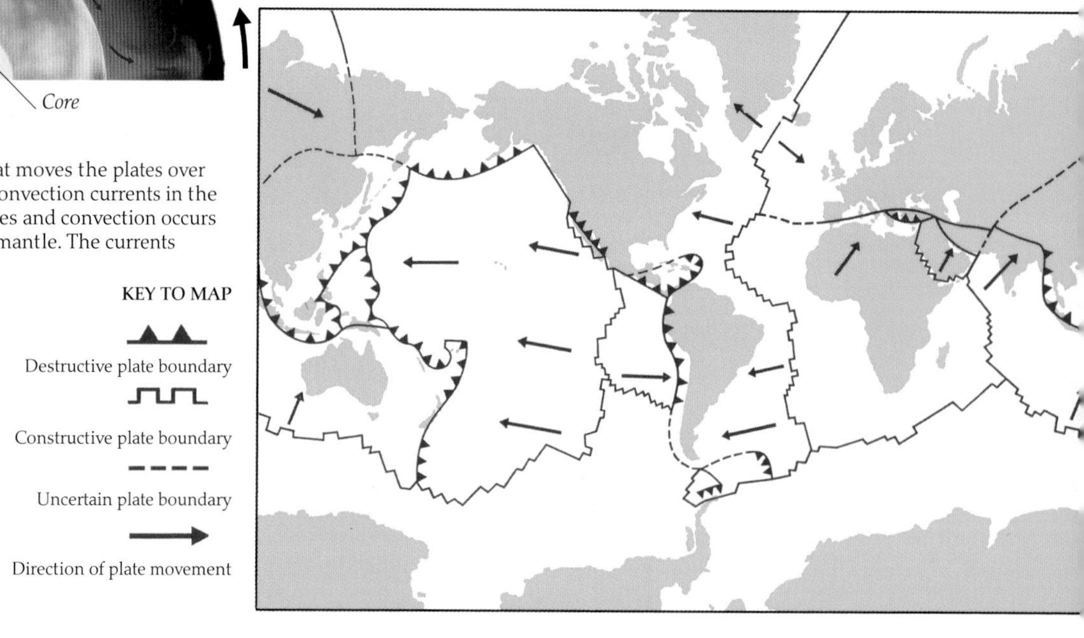
KEY TO MAP
Destructive plate boundary
Constructive plate boundary
Uncertain plate boundary
Direction of plate movement

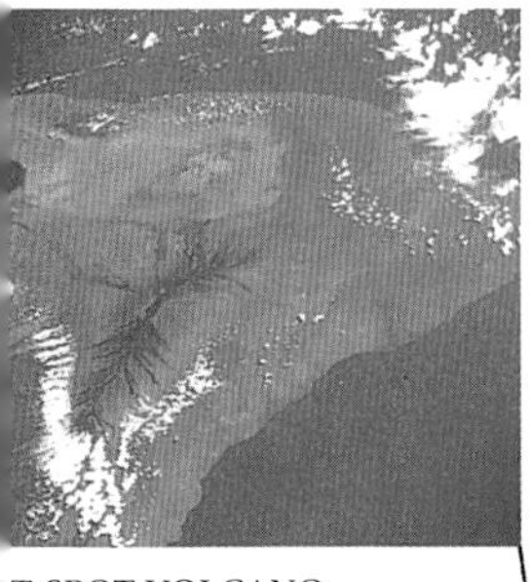

T-SPOT VOLCANO
waii, with some of the most ive volcanoes in the world, is at a plate boundary. There are ens of volcanic areas, not near e margins, where mantle-erated magma erupts through thickness of the plate. These hot spots (pp. 44–45).

Global relief map of North and South America

SAN ANDREAS REGION
At some plate boundaries, the plates slide past one another, in opposing directions or in the same direction at different speeds. There is no mechanism to produce magma, so there are no volcanoes. This is a boundary where plate is neither made nor destroyed (pp. 42–43).

ICELAND
At constructive plate boundaries, new oceanic plate is being made as magma emerges from the mantle. It fills a widening rift left as the plates move apart. Iceland is made of oceanic crust material, even though it is above sea level (pp. 38–39).

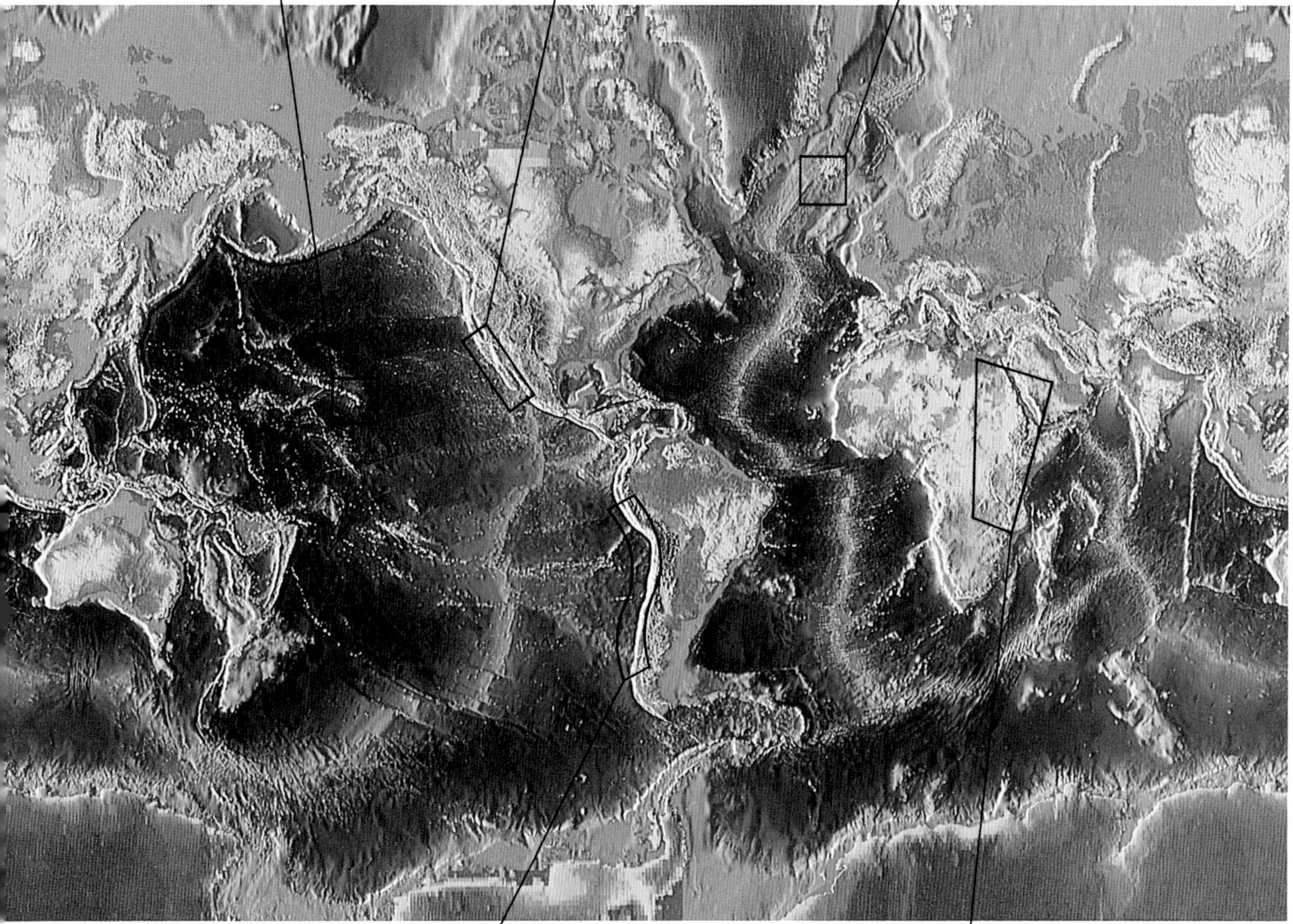

ANDES IN CHILE
Volcanoes, deep ocean trenches, and thquakes occur at the tructive plate margins ed subduction zones. Here, oceanic plate is nsumed or destroyed as it goes down into the mantle and is overridden by the neighboring plate (pp. 42–45).

AFRICAN RIFT VALLEY
Continents begin to split apart along rift valleys. In Africa, a branching rift extends southward from the Red Sea. This area was uplifted some 20 million years ago, and lava erupted. There are still many active volcanoes in this rift valley (pp. 48–49).

Map of mid-Atlantic Ridge

The formation of the ocean floor

HARRY HESS (1906–69)
An American geologist, Hess worked in submarines during World War II, where he was mapping the topography of the ocean floor. He found that the heat flowing from the ocean floor was much greater than expected. In 1960, he suggested that the ocean floor was young, because of the hot mantle rock continually rising and crystallizing at the ridges. He argued that the ocean floor was moving away from the ridges and was being consumed back into the mantle at the ocean trenches that surround the Pacific Ocean.

THE SURVEY SHIP *Challenger* (pp. 30–31) discovered that most of the ocean floor lies around 3 miles (5 km) below the surface. This deep ocean floor is all made of relatively young rocks, none older than 200 million years. There was ocean floor in earlier times, but all of that old rock has disappeared, subducted into the Earth's interior at destructive plate boundaries (pp. 36–37). New ocean floor is being made all the time by seafloor spreading, which takes place at midocean ridges. Here, magma rises from the mantle and fills the crack left as the ocean floor pulls apart. The uppermost layer of the volcanic ocean floor is basalt lava. Beneath this is a layer with vertical structures, and below this, a third layer made of coarse-textured gabbro. The Earth's magnetic field reverses its direction from time to time, and these reversals are recorded in the new ocean floor rocks as they crystallize.

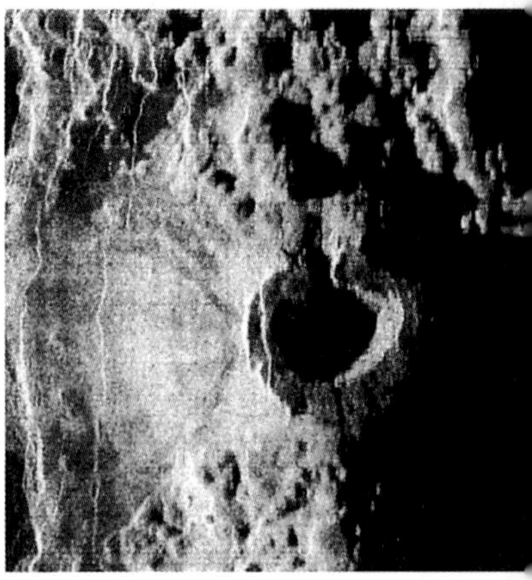

OCEAN-FLOOR VOLCANO
This sonar image shows a volcano on the Mid-Atlantic Ridge. Some ocean-floor volcanoes are active and produce enough la to make islands. Others, like this one, are w below sea level. A third extinct type have fla tops and are called guyots. Their tops were once at sea level, where the waves planed th flat. The ocean floor moved away from its spreading ridge, cooling and contracting as moved, carrying the guyot into deeper wate

BLACK SMOKERS
Hot springs at the spreading ridges emit water heated by the underlying magma. This water is seawater that has seeped into the new hot ocean floor as it cracks during cooling. The water gets hotter as it circulates through the hot rock, enabling it to dissolve more and more minerals from the rock it travels through. When the water is boiled out at the rift in the spreading ridge, it is full of metal sulfides in solution. As these come into contact with cold seawater, they come out of solution as black particles that build up into a smoker, a chimneylike structure that supports specially adapted animals (p. 10).

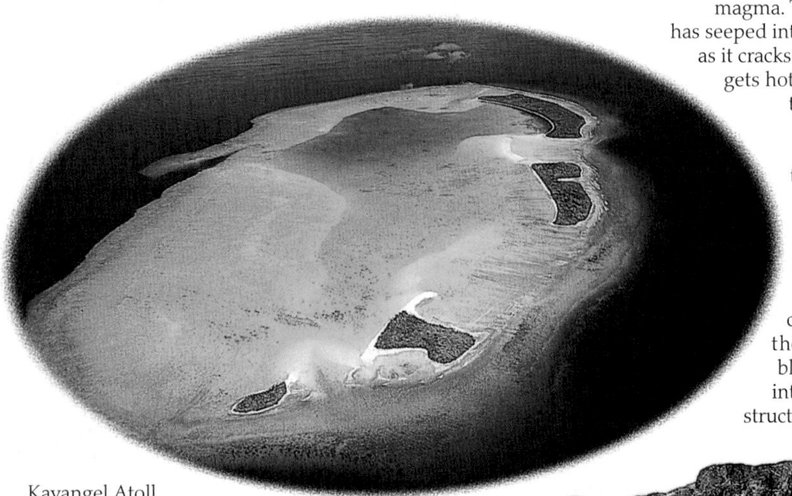

Kayangel Atoll
in the Pacific Ocean

CORAL ATOLLS
Coral atolls are ring-shaped islands constructed by reef-building corals. Charles Darwin (1809–82) showed them to be reefs around the fringes of extinct volcanic islands that had sunk below wave level. Many of these sunken islands turned out to be guyots—flat-topped mountains in the deep ocean. Harry Hess investigated why some guyots had no coral fringe. He realized that they sank beneath the depth of wave erosion (p. 54) as they were transported away from the hot, high ridges and some had sunk too fast for coral building to keep pace.

Manganese nodule

MINING THE OCEAN FLOOR
The deep ocean floor is littered with roundec nodules that contain the metal manganese. They are especially common where sedimer collects slowly. They grow gradually by adding another skin of metal around the outside and may join together, as here. Measurements of the ages of the rings from radiometric dating (p. 61) show that nodules grow extremely slowly. Their origin is in debate, but the metal content suggests that perhaps th is a connection with the metal sulfides of black smokers (above).

lapping the ocean

lowing the invention of echo-sounding
hniques, a ship can now chart the water
oth as it travels. More sophisticated
oth recording in the 1950s mapped
ocean floor and showed the diversity
the topography for the first time. The
ndings revealed volcanoes, rivers,
nches, and spreading ridges—the longest
ntinuous mountain chain on the Earth,
etching 40,400 miles (65,000 km).

OVE SEA LEVEL IN ICELAND
e amount of magma coming from the mantle
der Iceland is so great that a huge thickness of
a has built up the Icelandic landmass. Here,
ridge is above sea level. The central feature
the ridge in Iceland is a rift valley where
canic activity is greatest.

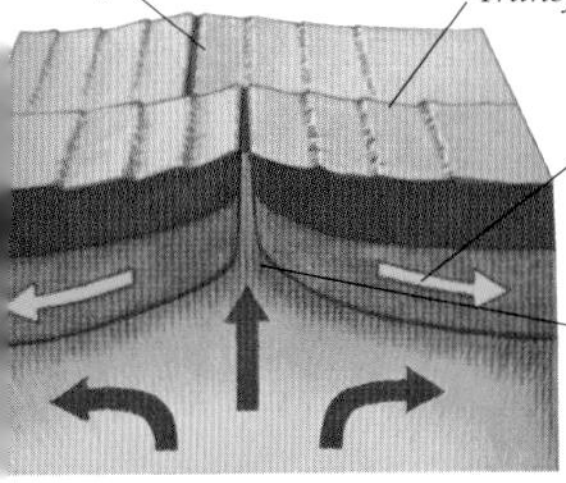
valley
Transform fault
Plate movement
Hot magma

W OCEAN FLOOR FORMS
t magma wells up under a crack—
ft valley—in the ocean. Some of
magma wells right up to the
bed and crystallizes as basalt lava.
me solidifies in the rift valley itself,
king a vertical wall parallel to
length of the rift valley. Some
idifies more slowly below.

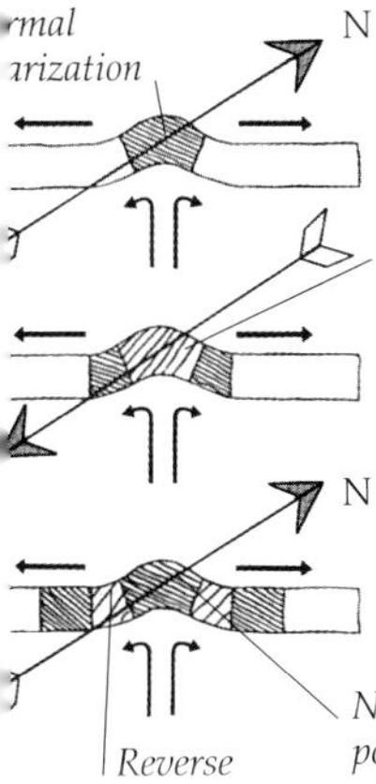
rmal
arization
N
Reverse polarization
N
Normal polarization
Reverse polarization

MAGNETIC STRIPES
Basalt lava contains minerals that align themselves in the direction of the Earth's magnetic field as they crystallize. The Earth's field reverses its direction from time to time, and the lavas preserve the direction of the field for the time when they crystallized. Over a long period, a whole series of stripes recording normal and reversed polarity events makes up the ocean floor (p. 61).

The Mid-Atlantic Ridge is above sea level in Iceland

THE MID-ATLANTIC RIDGE
This model of a section of the Mid-Atlantic Ridge was made from sonar images that map the ocean floor precisely. A series of parallel ridges develop as the rift valley cracks and widens, each length of rift wall slumping into the rift. In the center, the rift is shown at its deepest. The red represents hot lava welling up from the underlying mantle. Individual sections of the central rift are offset sideways by transform faults. These transform, or move, the ridge from one place to another.

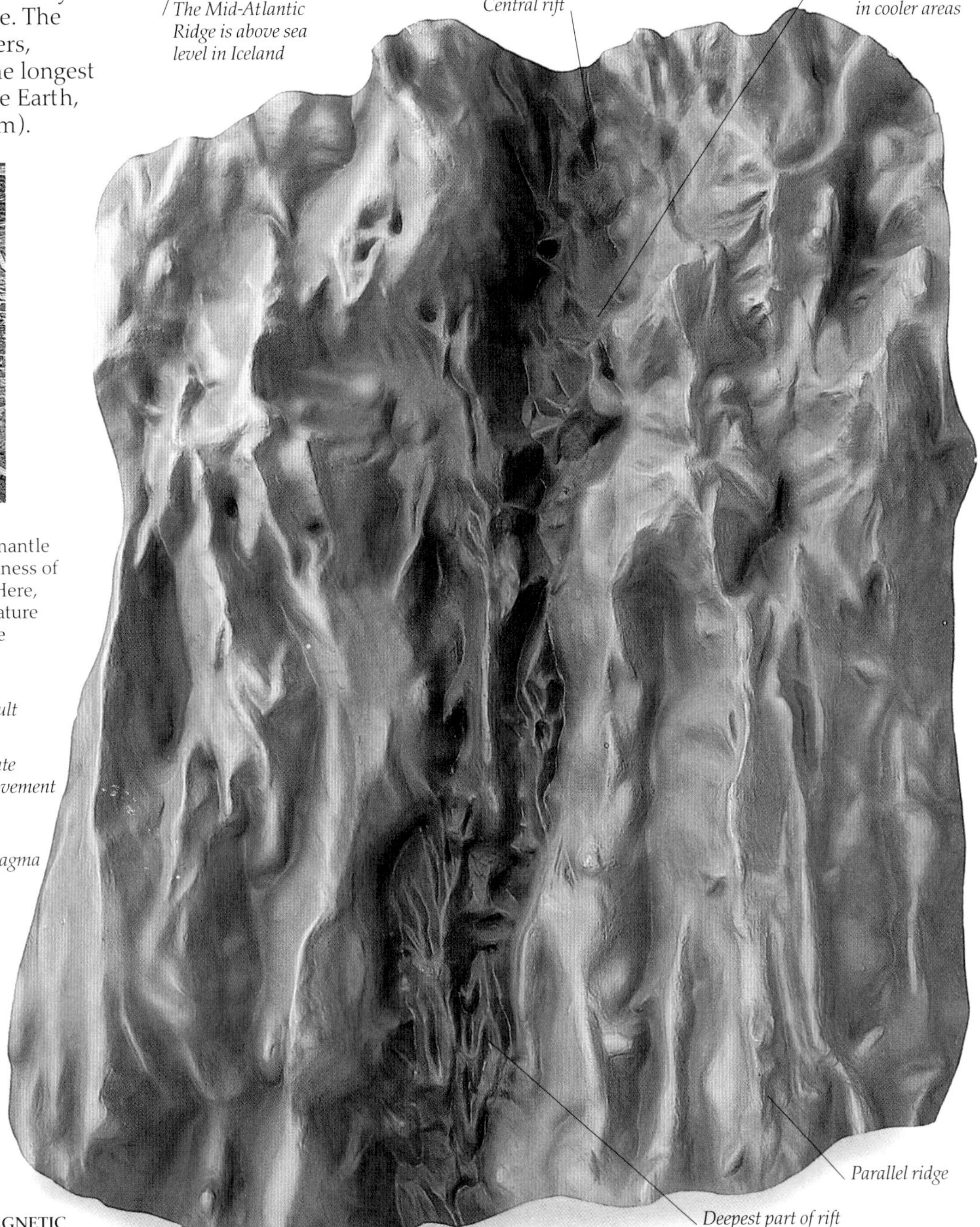
Central rift
Black smokers occur in cooler areas
Parallel ridge
Deepest part of rift
Parallel ridge

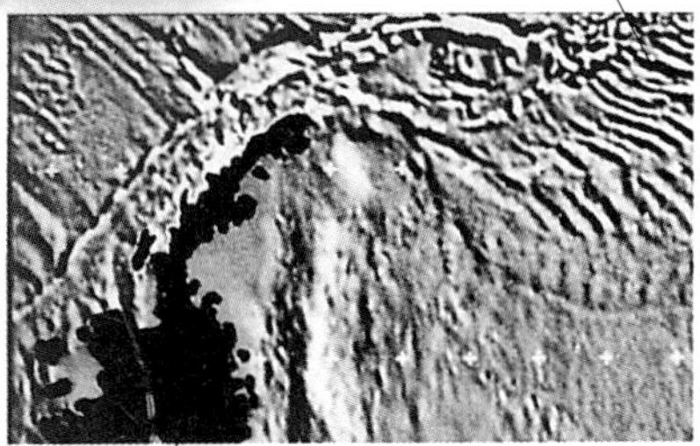
Antarctica

PLOTTING PLATE MOVEMENTS
This satellite image shows the topography, or shapes and structures, over a vast area of the ocean floor between Antarctica and South America. The conspicuous parallel ridges are old parts of the spreading ridge that surrounds the continent of Antarctica. Geologists use these shapes to determine the age and past movements of the plates.

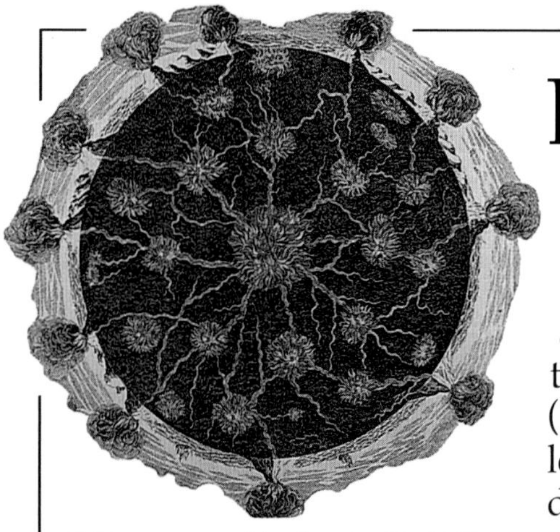

Subterranean world as imagined in 1665

Exploring the interior

THE EARTH'S INTERIOR may forever remain inaccessible (p. 32), but indirect methods have revealed that it has a layered structure wi an inner and outer core, surrounded by a mantle, and a crust around the outside. In 1910, the Croatian scientist Andrija Mohorovicic (1857–1936) concluded after studying transmission of waves from a local earthquake that there was a boundary about 22 miles (35 km) down. This is now called the Mohorovicic Discontinuity after him—shortened to Moho—and it marks the base of the crust. There are clues to the nature of the mantle and outer core. Volcanic eruptions bring some samples of mantle rocks to the surface and the chemistry of the mantle can be guessed at from the chemistry of basalt lavas that originate by partial melting of the mantle. Other indicators include earthquake waves, which travel at variable speeds through the interior of the Earth, depending on the density of the rock they pass through. Some kinds of waves are cut off altogether in the outer core, indicating it is liquid as far as wave transmission is concerned, in spite of the huge pressure at the core. By looking at the changes in the orbits of the planets and their moons as well as those of space satellites, it has been shown that the Earth's greatest mass is concentrated in the core.

HEAT FROM BELOW
Hot springs, which erupt violently as geysers, are visible proof that temperature increases with depth inside the Earth's crust. Miners have known this for many centuries. In the deepest modern gold mines in South Africa, the geothermal heat is so intense that the mines must be cooled to make any human activity possible at all.

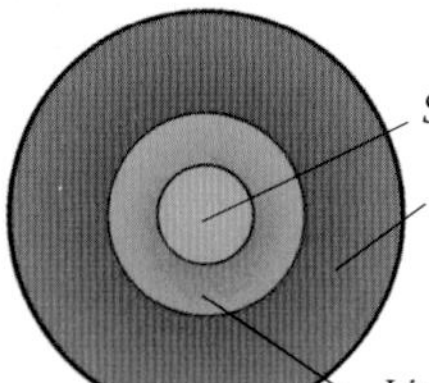

Solid iron inner core
Heavy silicates in mantle
Liquid iron outer core

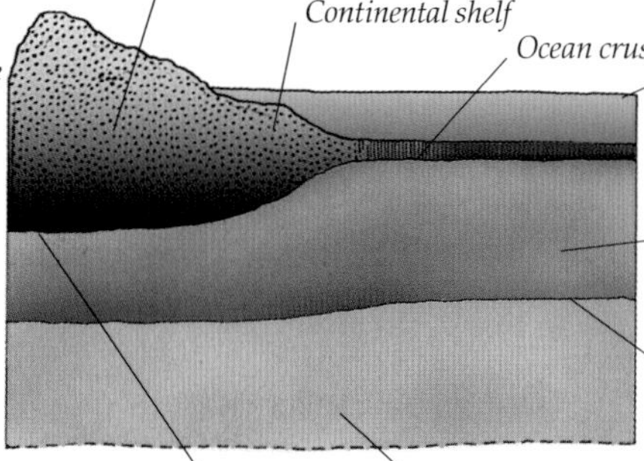

Continental crust
Continental shelf
Ocean crust
Sea level
Lithosphere
Base of lithosphere
Moho
Mantle

LAYERED EARTH
The plates that move around on the Earth's surface are made of more than the thickness of the crust. They include the uppermost part of the mantle. The plate is called lithosphere and is everywhere about 60 miles (100 km) thick. Oceanic lithosphere has oceanic crust at the top, which is only about 3 miles (5 km) thick. Continental lithosphere has continental crust above, which is thicker—22 miles (35 km).

Red garnet

Trucks send out vibrations
BMV 37Y

USING SEISMIC WAVES
Earthquake waves travel through the Earth, and their travel times can give information about the structure of the material they pass through. Vibrations can also be produced artificially to investigate inaccessible rocks at shallow depths. These special trucks give out a restricted range of vibrations that are picked up by listening devices, called geophones, situated various distances away.

GARNET PERIDOTI
Garnet peridotite, which l approximately the same density the mantle, is found at the Eart surface. Volcanic diamond-beari rocks called kimberlite cont garnet peridotite. To make diamo high pressure is needed, equivalent a depth of around 93 miles (150 k inside the Earth, so perhaps t garnet peridotite fragments the kimberlite are portions of t mantle from the same great dep

Eclogite

gite is
:d deep
he
t

Granite

gite on scales

ght
rams

WEIGH THE ROCK
The sample
clogite is
t weighed.

MEASURE VOLUME
To determine the
ume of a rock for
sity calculation, a
eka jar is filled with
er up to the point
ere water flows out
he spout. The rock is
n put gently inside.
volume of water
placed through the
ut is equivalent to
volume of the rock
ubic centimeters.

DENSE ROCKS
We cannot look at or touch the Earth's mantle directly, but some surface rocks have the same density, so it is possible that they have come from the mantle. The density of a rock gives a guide to what it might be made of. Crustal rocks from the continents have, on average, a density like that of granite—around 2.8. Mantle rocks are much denser, at 3.3. To find the density of a rock, the mass of the rock is compared to an equal volume of water.

Eclogite inside Eureka jar

Displaced water pours out into beaker

SIR WILLIAM LOGAN (1798–1875)
Traveling through uncharted terrain, Canadian-Scottish geologist William Logan first mapped the old rocks of the Canadian Shield (an area that has remained stable). He realized their great antiquity and that they represented rocks from the deepest levels of the Earth's crust. It is believed that these rocks, which make up the antique cores of continents, may underlie all the younger continental rocks. Knowledge of deep-level rocks is still sketchy, based on seismic work (p. 42) and on comparisons with the complicated metamorphic rocks (pp. 28–29) of the shield.

Lake Bonneville, Salt Lake City, Utah

BALANCING ACT
The thick, heavy ice sheets of the Pleistocene Ice Age depressed the surface rock layers of the crust beneath, and some of the mantle flowed out of the way. When the ice melted, the crust was unloaded and the mantle slowly flowed back to compensate for the loss of mass. The mantle flowed more slowly than the ice was melting, so Scandinavia is still rising today. This effect of the natural balancing between material of higher and lower density is called isostasy.

FLOATING CITY
Isostasy acts slowly, because the mantle flows slowly. Isostatic readjustment can be seen at the salt flats of Lake Bonneville, where Salt Lake City is built. The salt flats were once occupied by a vast, deep lake that has been considerably reduced. The area is still rising in isostatic adjustment to the removal of the weight of the water.

The weight causes the wood to float low in the water

The wood floats low in the water

e crust is depressed by the ice sheet like the wood with a weight on top

The weight is removed

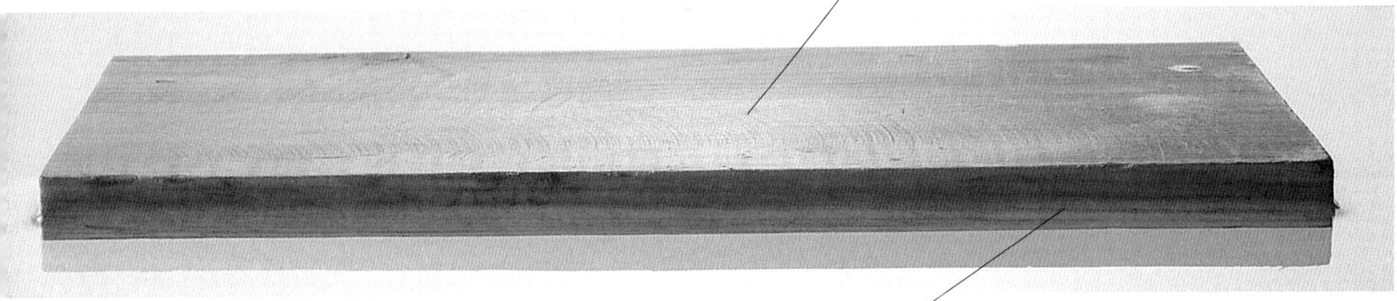

e continents float on the mantle like the wood on the water

The wood pops up

Earthquakes and seismology

JAPANESE INSTABILITY
Japan lies over a destructive plate boundary and consequently has many volcanic eruptions and great earthquakes. The land is rapidly being uplifted, making mountains, which themselves are rapidly eroding. The 2011 earthquake was one of the most devastating that Japan has suffered.

MOST LARGE EARTHQUAKES HAPPEN at plate boundaries, although a significant number originate in the middle of continental plates (p. 36). The majority of earthquakes go unnoticed by humans. In the buildup to an earthquake, stress accumulates in a volume of rock. The stress comes about because of the movement of the plates, whether slipping past one another or one plate subducting under the continental crust. At the point and time where stress exceeds the strength of the rock, fracture takes place. The fracture travels out through the region of stressed rock, and energy is released in all directions as seismic waves. Seismographs to measure earthquake shaking are highly sensitive devices, capable of recording earthquake waves from the far side of the globe. The traces recorded on seismographs can be read by seismologists to determine the location of a distant earthquake (its epicenter) and how energetic it was (its Richter magnitude). Intensity, based on the Mercalli scale, is compiled from eyewitness reports and from estimates of the response of buildings.

EDUARD SUESS (1831–1
An Austrian geologist, Suess theorized ab mountain ranges and their relationship each other. He did not believe that the E had evolved through a series of catastrop He saw the continents as stable regi making exception for the seis zones where earthquakes oc

GROUND CRACKS
Many people imagine that in an earthquake the ground cracks open and people or animals are swallowed up. This rare, but there is sometimes cracked groun and sometimes ground may liquefy durin shaking, especially where the underlyin rocks are loosely packed sediments and a saturated with water. During liquefactio heavy buildings may sink into the groun or buried objects, such as pipelines and even coffins, may rise to the surface. Landslides and avalanches may occur on steep slopes.

RECORDING APPARATUS
Early seismographs included a device for picking up the shaking. In addition, it was necessary to keep a written record of the shaking as well as to note the moment of arrival of the first tremor and the duration of shaking. The principle of a seismograph is that the recording part moves with the Earth, but a massive part of the apparatus stays stationary. In early equipment, the heavy, huge mass sometimes weighed many tons. The modern apparatus is small and inconspicuous and uses electronic circuitry.

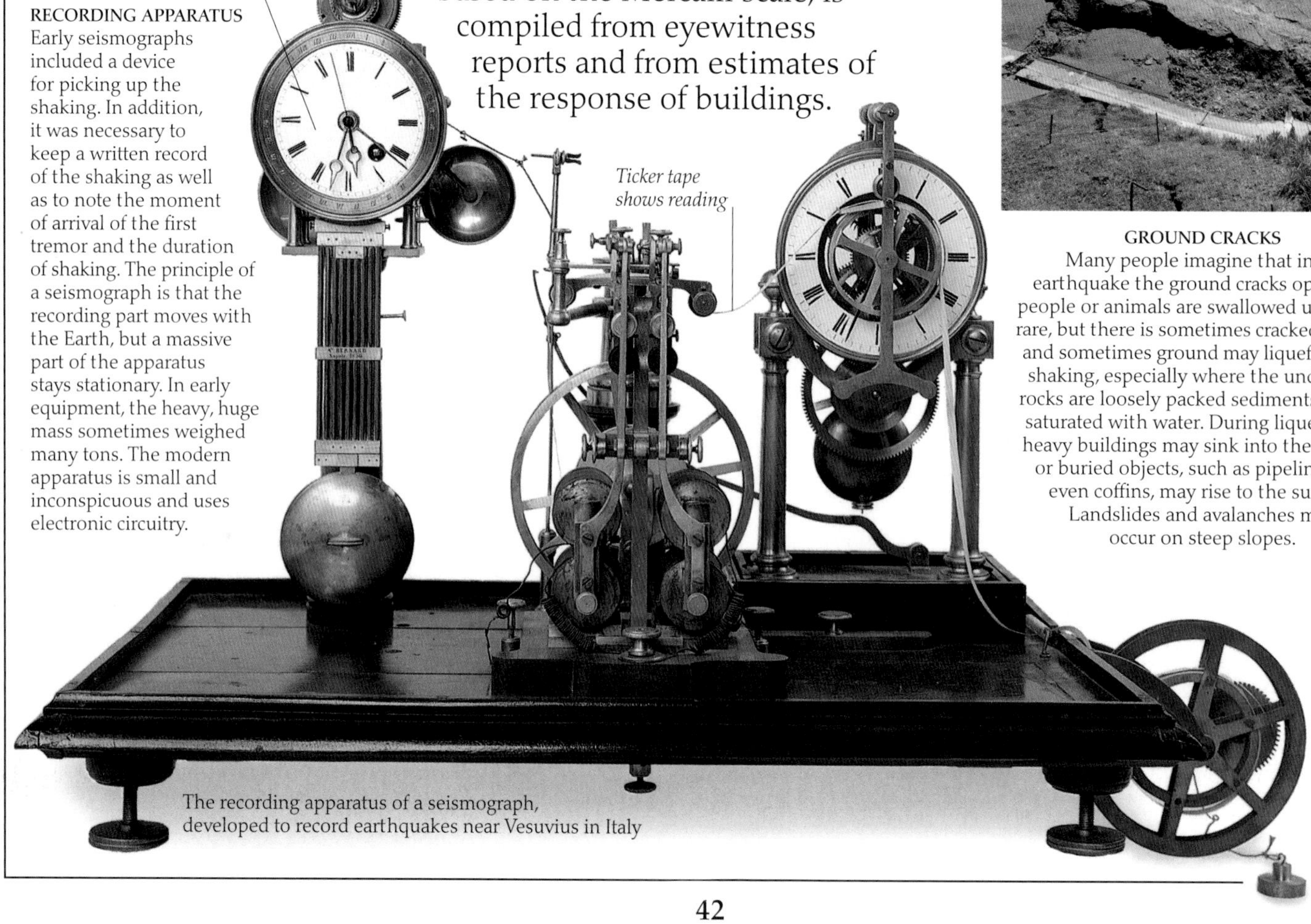

Clock mechanism stops when shaking starts
Ticker tape shows reading

The recording apparatus of a seismograph, developed to record earthquakes near Vesuvius in Italy

PRIMARY AND SHEAR WAVES

Earthquake waves travel outward in all directions. Some penetrate into the Earth, and their speed increases as they meet ever denser rocks so that they travel in ırved pathways and are refracted back up to the Earth's surface. Those that ɜnetrate to the core are slowed down ; they pass into the liquid outer core.)f these, the S waves, which transmit shearing the rocks they pass through, cannot travel through liquids and are t off. The primary waves (P waves) have a simpler motion so they travel faster and are the first to be recorded by a seismograph.

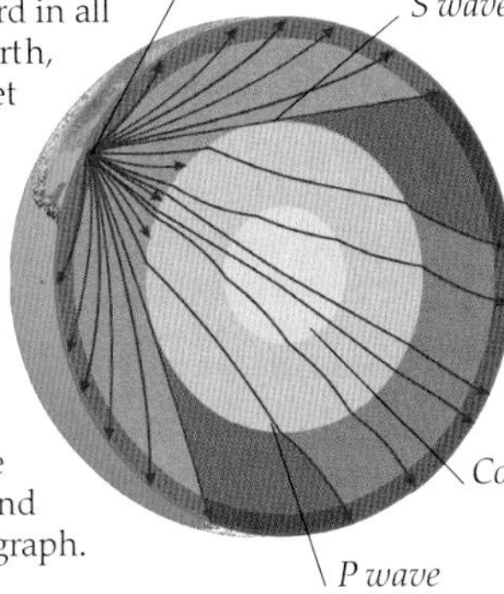

Epicenter
S wave
Core
P wave

San Andreas fault

The San Andreas earthquake zone is a complex of faults about 60 miles (100 km) wide. Here, the Pacific plate is moving northwestward in relation to the landmass of continental North America, so that the relative motion along the boundary is sideways. At these plate boundaries, or margins, plate is neither being made (pp. 36–37), nor consumed.

North America

The San Andreas fault on the west coast of the US

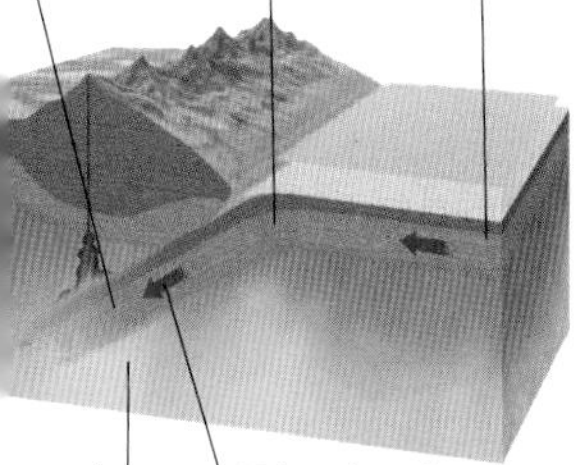

thquakes
r
Subduction zone
Oceanic crust
Mantle
Direction of convection currents

SUBDUCTION ZONES

Earthquakes are concentrated in sloping zones that underlie mountain ranges and island arcs. Plate tectonics (pp. 36–37) explains that these happen where the oceanic crust is carried down (subducted) into the mantle. The greatest depth at which earthquakes originate is 425 miles (700 km). It is assumed that below this depth, the cold descending lithosphere slab has been heated so much in the mantle that it is no longer brittle enough to fracture.

River has been moved sideways by fault
Fault line
Highway

FAMOUS FAULT LINE

Earthquake shaking is less intense the farther away it is from the focus, the point where the earthquake originates below the epicenter. Deep earthquakes generally cause less shaking at the Earth's surface above. All the earthquakes on the San Andreas fault are shallow—they originate less than 19 miles (30 km) down.

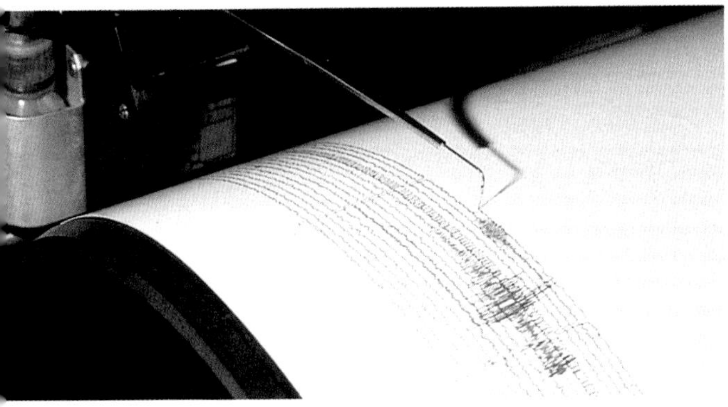

ORDING EARTHQUAKES

ɜismometer records the movement he ground at strategic points. These dings may be transmitted by radio or ·phone line to a recording station. ɛ, a paper record shows one ıponent of the ground motion.

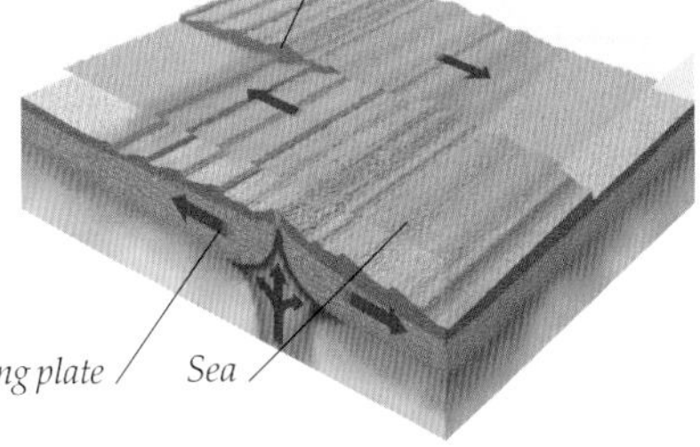

Transcurrent fault where plates slip past one another
Moving plate
Sea

TRANSCURRENT FAULT

Faults that move predominantly sideways are called transcurrent faults. Along some sections of the San Andreas Fault movement is almost continuous. In other places it is locked, and stress builds up, leading to large earthquakes.

PULLING THE EARTH APART

Some faults occur because rock is under tension. This model (below) shows how faults develop in a series of layered sedimentary rocks. As the layers are stretched, there comes a time when the strength of the rock is no longer able to hold the rock together.

Layers of sand represent sedimentary rock and are colored so faults can be clearly seen
Fault line
Faulting occurs on either side of rift

Volcanology

AN ERUPTING VOLCANO is one of the most spectacular of all natural phenomena. The lava that erupts from a volcano is a hot silicate liquid containing gas. Its viscosity varies enormously. Some lava is very fluid and flows freely. Other lavas are so viscous that the lava barely flows at all, and instead heaps up around the hole in the ground and builds a dome. If there is a long time interval between eruptions—for instance, hundreds or even thousands of years—the entire top of the volcano may be blown to dust in a major explosion. Most volcanoes occur in chains that follow the plate boundaries. The formulation of the plate tectonics theory (pp. 36–37) helped to explain the mystery of why volcanoes are not dotted randomly around the globe. Many are to be found around the shores of the Pacific Ocean and in a belt through the Mediterranean to Indonesia. Some volcanoes are at subduction zones (p. 43), where ocean floor moves down into the mantle and is partly melted, making magma (p. 25). Others occur at the spreading ridges where they make new ocean floor (p. 39). Other locations are in rift valleys where continents first began to split apart (p. 49).

THE GRACEFUL MONSTER
Mount Vesuvius in Italy erupted in 79 CE. Before the eruption the sides of the volcano were lushly covered in vines. Roman cities on its slopes were engulfed by hot ash. The less-devastating 1872 eruption is shown here.

Icelandic
Hawaiian
Strombolian
Vulcanian
Pelean
Plinian

CLASSIFY
ERUPTI
Eruptions are descr
according to the explosivene
their activity. This ranges from
mildest outpourings of syrupy la
vigorous eruptions where magma g
escape in intermittent explos
or in clouds of hot

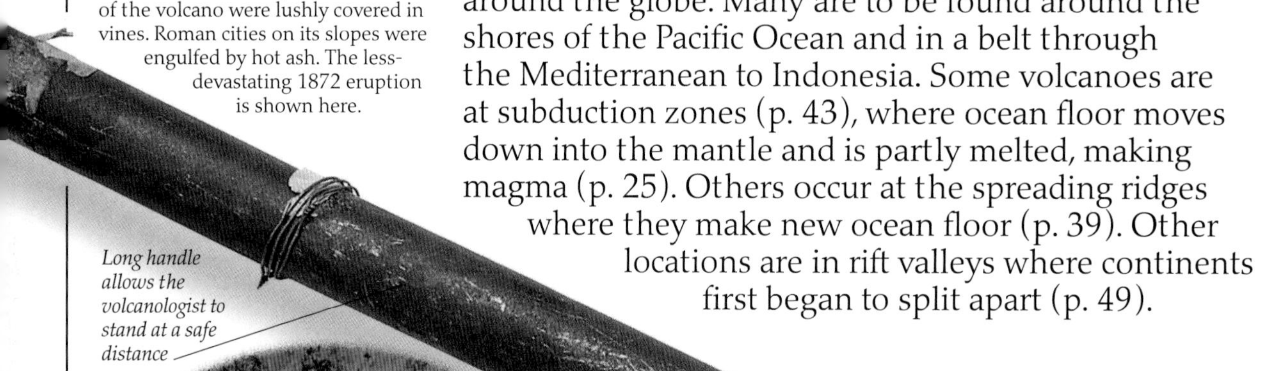

Long handle allows the volcanologist to stand at a safe distance
The twisted metal hook picks up lava from the flow
Twisted shape

COLLECTING LAVA
Many changes take place in lava as it cools and solidifies. Volcanologists (scientists who study volcanoes) watch events during an eruption and collect samples. Sampling helps to understand magma formation and to predict how far flows of lava will travel, and how quickly. This metal rod is used for collecting hot lava.

STUDYING VOLCANOES
Observing at an active volcano can be dangerous. To get close to the action, special heat-resistant clothing must be worn. While this protects from heat, gas, and falling lava blobs, it also hinders the volcanologist's freedom of movement. To describe an eruption, a volcanologist uses the classifications of eruption type (above right), which are internationally understood. This photograph shows a volcanologist in front of fire fountaining in a Hawaiian-type eruption, taking place in Iceland.

Lava bomb
Rough, vesicular surface

LAVA BC
Fragm
of lava that
thrown out in
fountains are still molte
they fly through the air. T
cool as they fall, taking
shape molded by their fli

awaiian volcanoes

e Hawaiian islands are the tops of a
ıin of volcanic islands situated over
ot spot in the mantle that has been
ɔducing magma for the last 6 million
ırs. The site of volcanic activity at
surface appears to have moved, but
ually the hot spot in the mantle stays
l; it is the Pacific plate that moves,
rying each volcano northwestward.

Asia
North America
Pacific Ocean
Hawaiian island chain

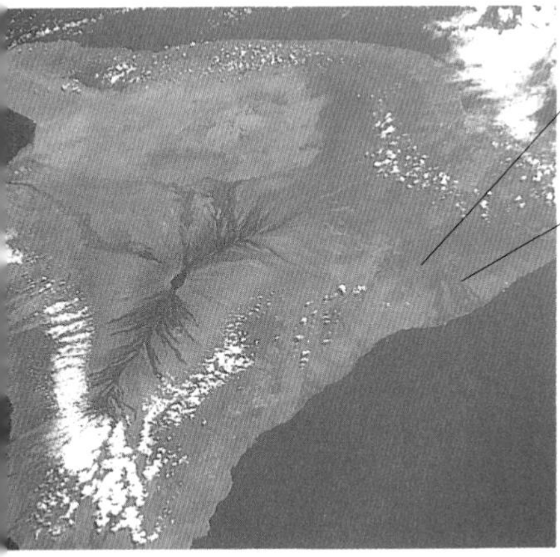
The core of Kilauea
New lava

E LARGEST VOLCANO
the "Big Island" of Hawaii, lava poured from
volcano Kilauea for a decade, beginning in
early 1980s. The southern slopes of the
nd became carpeted with new lava. The island
ually grew as lava flowed into the sea, making
v land. Above sea level, the whole island is
y the top of a cluster of massive volcanoes
ng from the Pacific ocean floor. Altogether,
entire complex is 32,800 ft (10,000 m) high,
king it the tallest mountain (from seafloor
summit) on Earth.

ROPY LAVA
Highly fluid lava cools with a continuous glassy skin over the surface. The internal flow may push up the cooled skin into wrinkles resembling strands of rope.

Wrinkled surface

Ropy lava from a Hawaiian eruption

LAVA FLOW
The popular image of volcanoes is a cone-shaped mountain with a crater on top where lava flows out from time to time. In fact, some are mere cracks in the ground, of which many occur in the ocean where lava pours out to cover the seabed. The fast-flowing lava eruptions are less dangerous to humans than those with thick viscous lava that erupt explosively. These can bury towns under thick layers of ash.

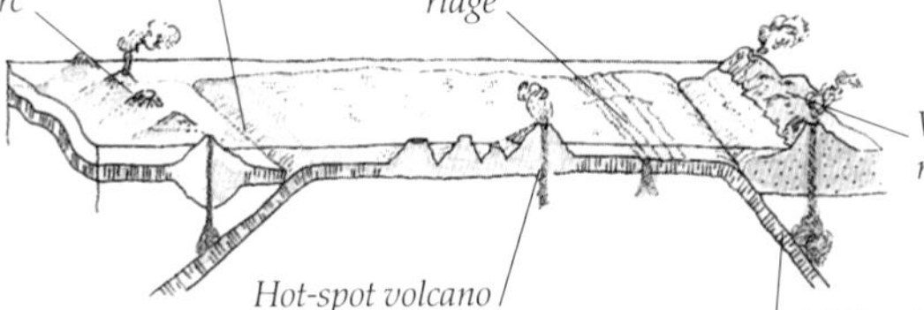
Island arc
Trench
Spreading ridge
Volcanic mountain chain
Hot-spot volcano
Subduction zone

VOLCANOES AND PLATE TECTONICS
Most volcanoes occur at plate boundaries. A few, some of them the largest and most active on the Earth, are in midplate locations. These, such as the Hawaiian volcanoes, are the hot-spot volcanoes. As the plate moves over the hot spot, a chain of volcanic islands forms, getting older the farther they are from the hot spot.

icular lava from a
vaiian-type eruption

Gas bubble (vesicle)

ICULAR LAVA
en magma erupts, volcanic gas comes
bling out from the liquid. Bubbles
he middle of the cooling lava
not escape, so eventually
lava hardens with the
-filled holes.

Mountain building

CROSSING THE ALPS
The Swiss physicist and explorer Horace-Bénédict de Saussure (1740–99) crossed the Alps 17 times in different places to try to understand how mountain ranges were created. In the end, he decided that mountains were hopelessly complex and that understanding their structure was impossible.

GEOLOGISTS ONCE THOUGHT that the folded structures in mountain ranges showed that the Earth was shrinking, and they likened mountain ranges to wrinkles on a shriveling apple. It is now known that mountain ranges are made up of rocks that have been stacked up and deformed into complicated structures, and that the Earth is not shrinking because new crust is being made in the oceans all the time (pp. 38–39). Usually there is more than one generation of deformation in the making of a mountain range, so that folds become refolded. Broad common features of mountain ranges are that the foothill rocks are recognizably sedimentary (pp. 26–27), while the middle of the ranges have more complicated rocks and structures—these rocks may be intensely deformed and recrystallized (pp. 24–25). Young mountain ranges at active plate boundaries (pp. 36–37) may have volcanoes sitting atop all the deformed structures. There is certainly a great deal of crushing and shortening of the crust in mountain building. However, deformation and uplift in themselves do not create the jagged peaks that are recognizably mountains. Erosion (pp. 54–55) of many miles' thickness of rock from the top of the rising landmass exposes the deep core of the mountain range. The entire process that makes mountain ranges is called orogenesis.

Upper parts of fold have been eroded
Sediment layers used to be horizontal

FOLD MOUNTAINS
Mountains show layers of sediment that have been folded into complex shapes. These vertical strata in southern England were folded at the same time as the Alps were formed a long way to the south.

THE ROCKY MOUNTAINS
In the late 19th century, it was assumed that some of the crustal shortening of mountain ranges was brought about by one set of rocks being pushed over another. This is called thrust faulting and it involves large-scale, near-horizontal movements of the upper crustal layers. This seemed like a farfetched idea, but it turned out to be right. The structures in the Rocky Mountains involve multiple thrusting, one mass on top of another. It is hard to imagine how these great movements could be happen in material as hard and brittle as rock. The upper section of rock that is pushed in thrust faulting is called a nappe.

The Rocky Mountains in North America

Simple deformation of sedimentary rock
Foothills

DELING MOUNTAINS
hard to understand how the nplicated structures that logists map in the field have ne into being. Simplified models nountain ranges forming from tinental collisions can be made laboratory. A machine spreads ored sand in a tank. A paper sheet olled slowly underneath the sand, ucing the length of the layers to tate subduction (p. 43).

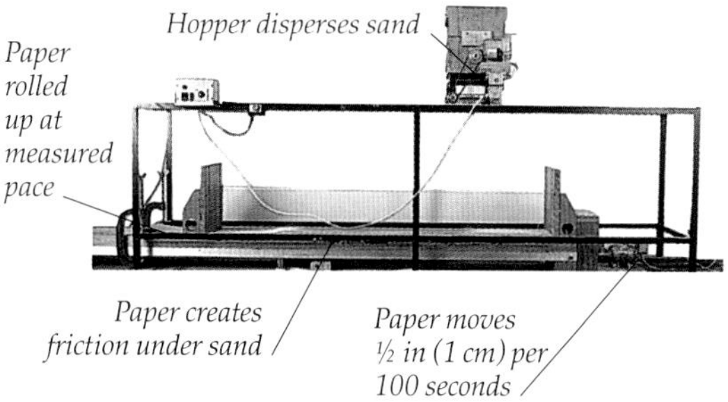

Hopper disperses sand
Paper rolled up at measured pace
Paper creates friction under sand
Paper moves ½ in (1 cm) per 100 seconds

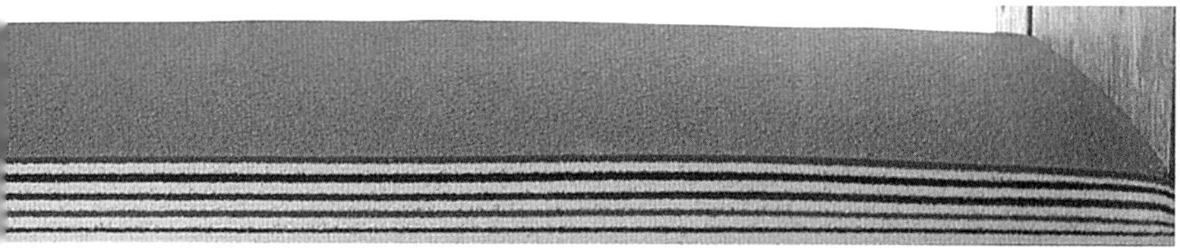

iments are laid down

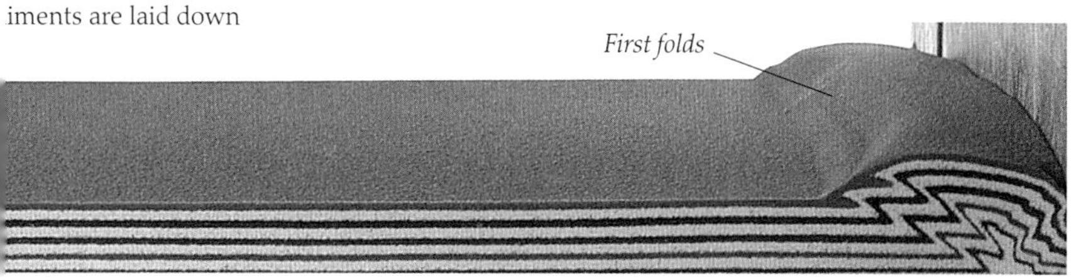

First folds

naped folds develop as the er is moved at a steady rate

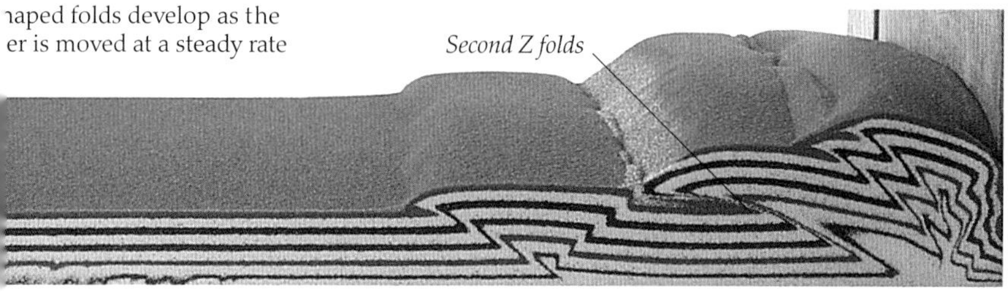

Second Z folds

v folds begin to form; the first are more intensely deformed

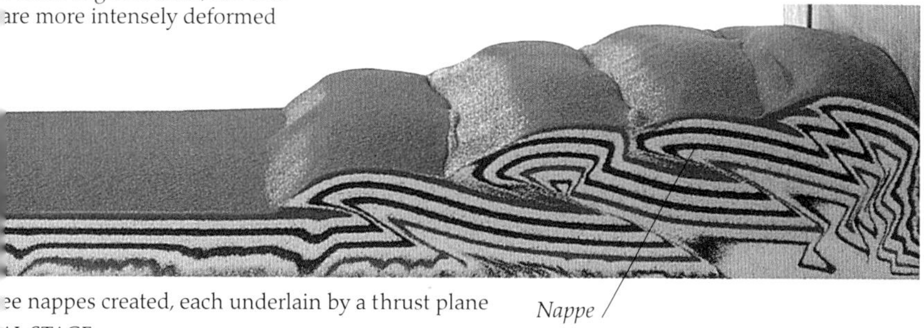

Nappe

ee nappes created, each underlain by a thrust plane

AL STAGE
ries of thrusts has placed one nappe on top of another. model only represents part of what happens in nature. eality, uplifting, folding, and thrust faulting accompanied by ion, intrusions, volcanoes.

Nappe
Thrust plane

The Andes

There are many signs of continuing uplift and other tectonic activity in the Andes. Many of the world's largest earthquakes originate here. Young marine sediments are found high above sea level, showing that uplift has been rapid. The Andes are distinctive for the large number of active volcanoes that make up many of the highest peaks. These are built above the mountain range itself. The volcanoes have produced great level spreads of ash, making up the elevated plateau of the altiplano.

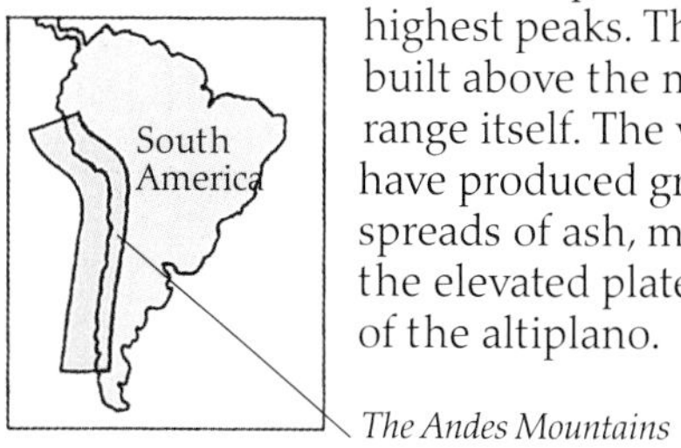

South America
The Andes Mountains

MOUNTAINS IN CHILE
The jagged nature of mountains comes about from erosion of land that has been raised by thrust faulting and deformation in orogenesis.

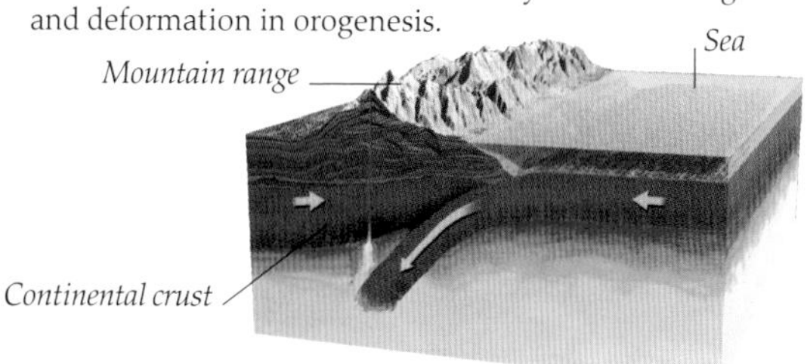

Mountain range
Sea
Continental crust

DESTRUCTIVE PLATE BOUNDARIES
The destructive plate movement in the Andes occurs when oceanic crust subducts beneath the continental crust. Sediments from the ocean floor are scraped off and added to the continent.

Plateaux and rifts

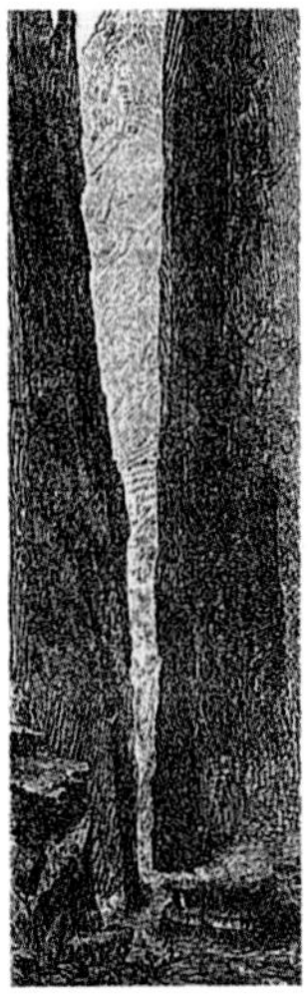

AUSTRIAN CANYON
A canyon is a deep valley with vertical sides that has been worn away and eroded by river water. The Austrian Alps show many such slotlike canyons in limestone.

A TOTALLY NEW PLATE BOUNDARY appears when a continent starts to rift apart. This happened 200 million years ago when the Atlantic Ocean first began to grow (pp. 38–39). Today, the continent of Africa is splitting apart along the African Rift Valley to make a new plate boundary. Not all rift valleys become oceans. Some remain as rifts to fill up with thick layers of igneous rocks and sediments. Some plateaux form when continents collide with each other. This happens when there is no more oceanic crust between them to be subducted. Unlike oceanic crust, continental crust does not subduct because it is too light in weight. So if the edges of continents collide, there is major crushing instead of one plate slipping under the other, and this forms a high plateau like the Tibetan Plateau. Other plateaux come about by gentle raising of a whole region.

JOHN WESLEY POWELL (1834–1[illegible]
Powell was an American who explored the Grand Can[illegible] in 1869. He had lost his right arm in the Civil War, managed to climb the canyon walls in places and hel[illegible] navigate his boats through the fast-flowing waterw[illegible]

RIFTING MODEL
The laboratory model below demonstrates the results of rifting. The layers show the fractures that cause rift valleys, sometimes with several more or less parallel faults, each of which allows the rift area to drop farther down. The rift section is sometimes known as a graben. In between the dropped blocks are regions that have stayed high. These are called horsts.

THE GRAND CANYON
The great thickness of sedim[illegible] that make up the Colorado Plateau have been lifted 10,000 ft (3,000 m) over the [illegible] 60 million years. Powell's tea[illegible] realized that the Grand Cany[illegible] showed no signs of glaciatio[illegible] The only explanation was that the river had eroded out the huge canyon, cutting first through the softer sediments and—at the botto[illegible] of today's canyon—through metamorphic rocks and grani[illegible]

Red and white sand shows the sedimentary layers formed at the same time as rifting

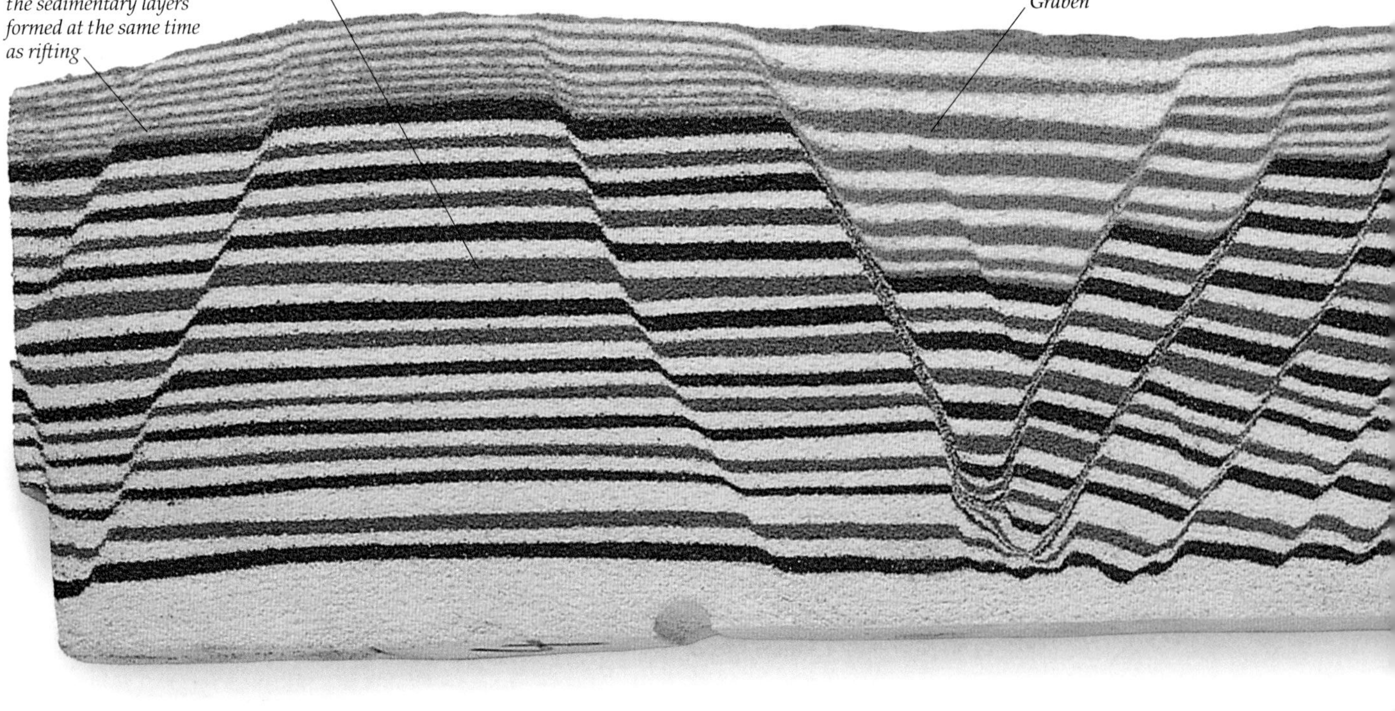

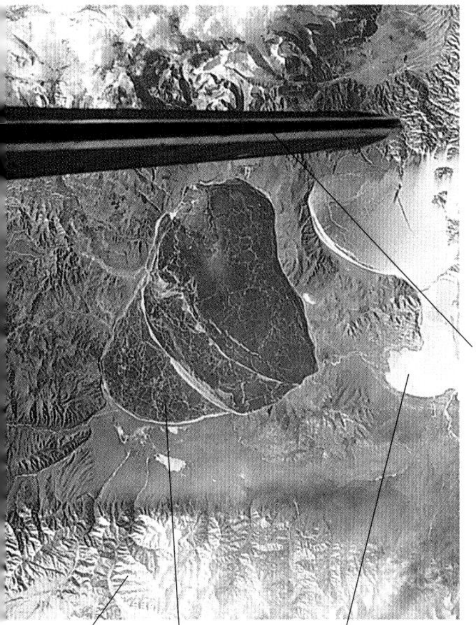
Satellite antenna
ntains
Plateau lake
Plateau lake

TIBETAN PLATEAU
highest level region on Earth is the Tibetan
eau, at 14,760 ft (4,500 m) above sea level. It is
ounded by young mountains to which its origins
inked. Other plateaux, like some in Africa, are
close to young mountain ranges; they seem to
formed from simple uplift.

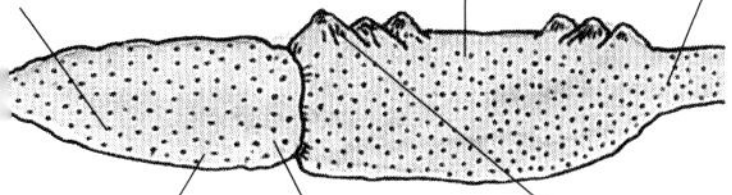
Plateau
Asia
kened
crust
Land
masses collide
Himalayas
formed

NCHING LANDMASSES
ng the last 10 million years, India has moved
hward into Asia after the total subduction
3) of the Tethys Ocean that lay between the
landmasses. As they collided, Asia became
pressed, deformed, and fractured, creating
Himalayan Mountains. The interior began
ompress to make the Tibetan Plateau.

African Rift Valley

Running through east Africa from Mozambique to the Red Sea is a great rifted valley that branches into two parts. Here, Africa is splitting apart along faults, where the continental lithosphere (p. 40) has broken right through. Young, active volcanoes and many earthquakes show that the rift is active. At the north, where the Rift Valley joins the Red Sea at the Danakil Depression, the floor of the rift is below sea level and made of oceanic crust, but it is still land. Farther south, none of the rock in the African section has oceanic crust. Sometime in the future, a new ocean may separate eastern Africa from the rest of the continent.

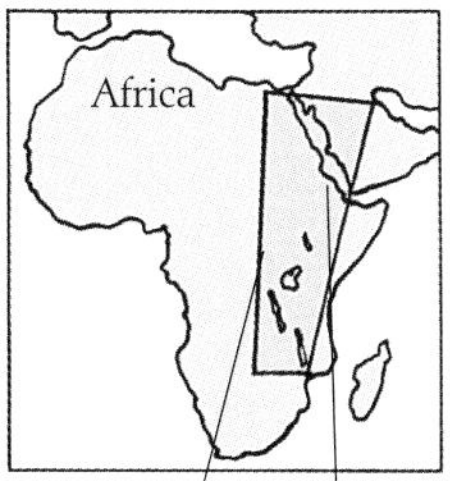
Africa
The African
Rift valley
Danakil Depression

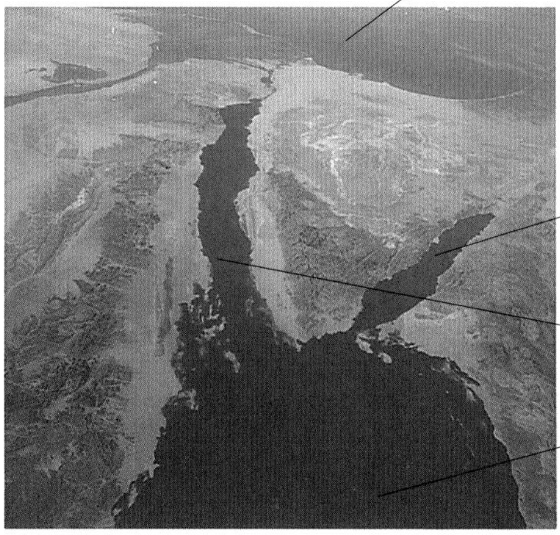
Mediterranean
Sea
Gulf of
Aqaba
Gulf
of Suez
Red
Sea

Satellite view of the Gulfs of Suez and Aqaba and the Red Sea

KENYAN RIFT SECTION
Rift valleys have volcanoes within the rift, and usually great spreads of basalt lava on the plateaulike areas on either side. The faultlines running along the Great Rift Valley in Kenya can be clearly seen in this aerial photograph.

A MINIATURE OCEAN
Gravity and magnetic surveys of the Red Sea revealed that the submarine sediments were underlain by oceanic crust. Surveys showed there was a pattern of magnetic stripes (p. 39) parallel to the length of the Red Sea; from these, the spreading rate can be calculated at 1 in (2.5 cm) per year. As the Red Sea spreads, so Arabia is moving northeastward, away from Africa and closing up the sea of the Persian Gulf.

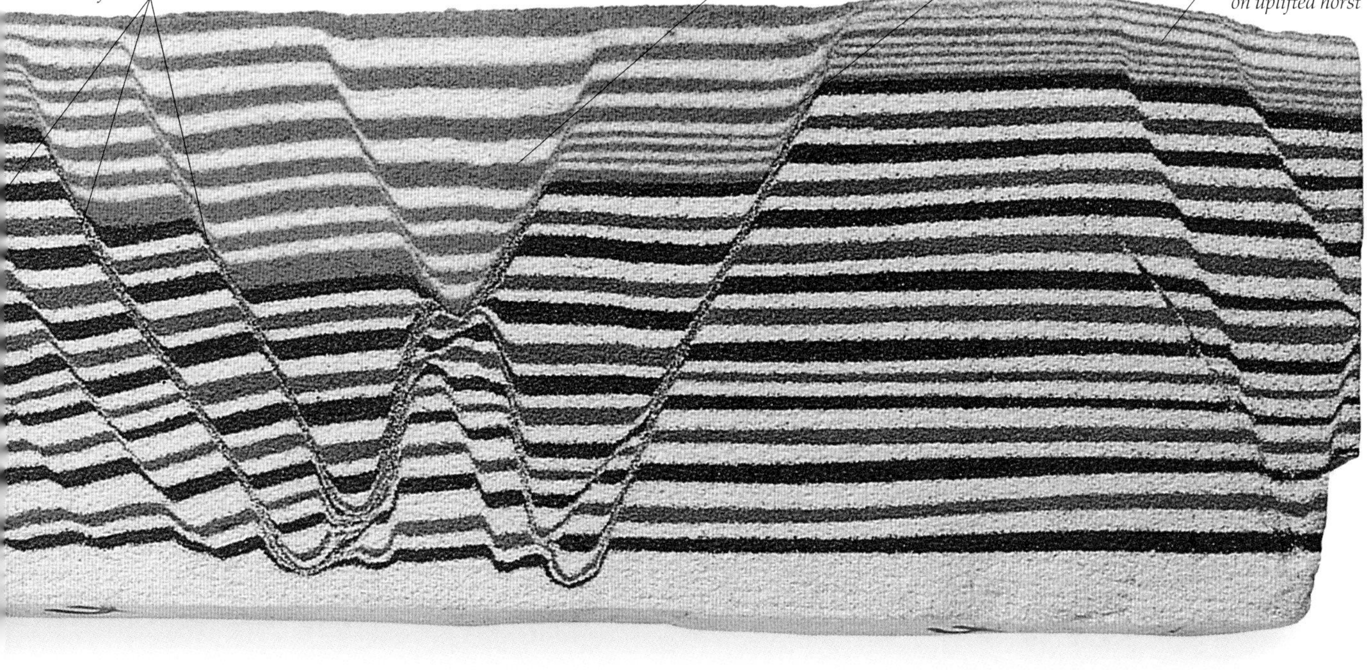
Parallel faults
Thickened red and
white layers in
the graben
Fracture
Thinner
sediment layers
on uplifted horst

Weathering processes

MANY OF THE MINERALS in rocks are stable at the high temperatures and pressures deep in the crust (pp. 40–41), but they are chemically unstable in the oxygen-rich atmosphere of the Earth. Rocks react chemically with the Earth's damp atmosphere in a process called weathering, which takes place right at the Earth's surface. This process contributes to the evolution of landforms. Some weathering is purely chemical—for example, the action of slightly acidic rain on limestone (p. 17). Temperature may also play a role in weathering. During the day, rock may be heated by the Sun. When the temperature drops at night, this change leads to stresses and cracking in the rocks. This will be made more extreme if water freezes in the cracks (pp. 58–59). Plants and animals, lichens, and fungi also help these processes along. None of these effects, however, happens in isolation. Most landscapes are the result of a combination of many weathering processes. Rock minerals are separated and changed by weathering; this weathered material may be transported and deposited somewhere else (pp. 56–57).

PLANT ACTION
Plant roots penetrate through cracks in rock and take in rock chemicals to use in their metabolism. As roots grov thicker and the plant bigger, the crack in the rock are widened. Trees help weathering. So do mosses and lichens which have fungal roots that can penetrate the hardest rocks.

RUSTING ROCK
Isolated hills, relics of an older, higher surface, may stand above a younger land surface that is almost a level plain. These isolated mountains are known as inselbergs. The red color of Uluru (Ayers Rock) in central Australia is due to iron oxides, the insoluble compound left behind after silicates are broken down by the Australian climate.

ANIMAL ACTION
Animals such as rabbits and badgers, as well a smaller creatures like beetles, burrow and ma channelways in the weathered rock zone whe solid rock comes into contact with moist air. This increases the rate of weathering, because it increases the surface area of the rock. This weathered rock is called saprolite.

CHANGES IN TEMPERATURE
The rocks in these Utah canyons are weathered by temperature, wind, and water. Changes in temperature cause cracking as the rocks expand and shrink. If an area gets very cold and freezing follows rain, the rainwater that has percolated into cracks and in between rock grains expands as it freezes, breaking the rock apart.

ıytor on
ırtmoor,
uthern
itain

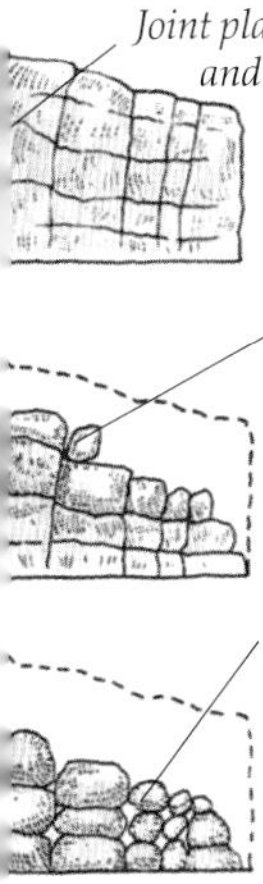

Joint planes develop and weathering takes place
Erosion leaves corestones
Granite tor

GRANITE TOR

Cooled granite eventually comes to the surface when a mountain range is being eroded away; the granite cracks apart as the load of rock over the top gets less and less. In places, the cracks, called joints, are spaced far apart. In other places, they are close together. Weathering of granite is most intense where the joints are closely spaced. This leaves rounded corestones of unweathered granite, some of which may be several yards or even hundreds of feet across. The more solid rock stands out as high areas of bare rock known as granite tors.

ION SKINS

athering begins the outside of ɔck, where it greatest contact h the atmosphere. athering processes ıetrate at least ½ in ːm) into the rock, even ere erosion is rapidly ıoving the weathered ins. On some rocks, several ıs of weathered rock can seen peeling off from the lerlying, more solid rock. s type of weathering ometimes called on-skin weathering, ɜxfoliation.

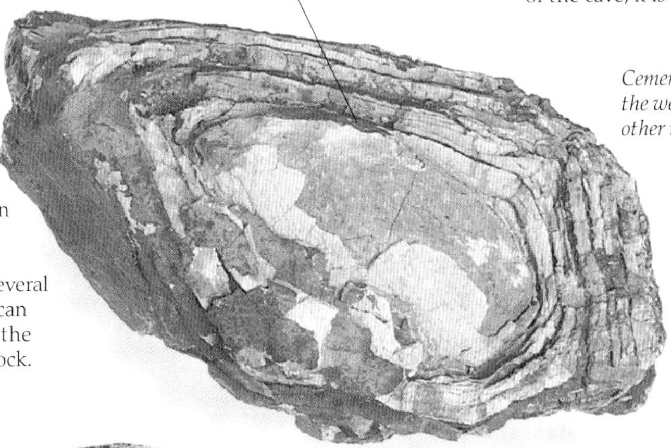

Peeling layers

Dolerite rock

LIMESTONE WONDER

Limestone is weathered by carbon dioxide in rainwater so that the rock is slowly eaten away. When water carrying the dissolved limestone drips from the roof of a cave, a stalactite forms. If the soil above the cave is an iron-rich clay, the stalactite may be red in color.

LIMESTONE LAGOON

The stalactites in this cave on Phra Nang Peninsula, Thailand, were exposed to daylight when the cave collapsed. If the limestone dissolved in water grows up from the floor of the cave, it is known as a stalagmite.

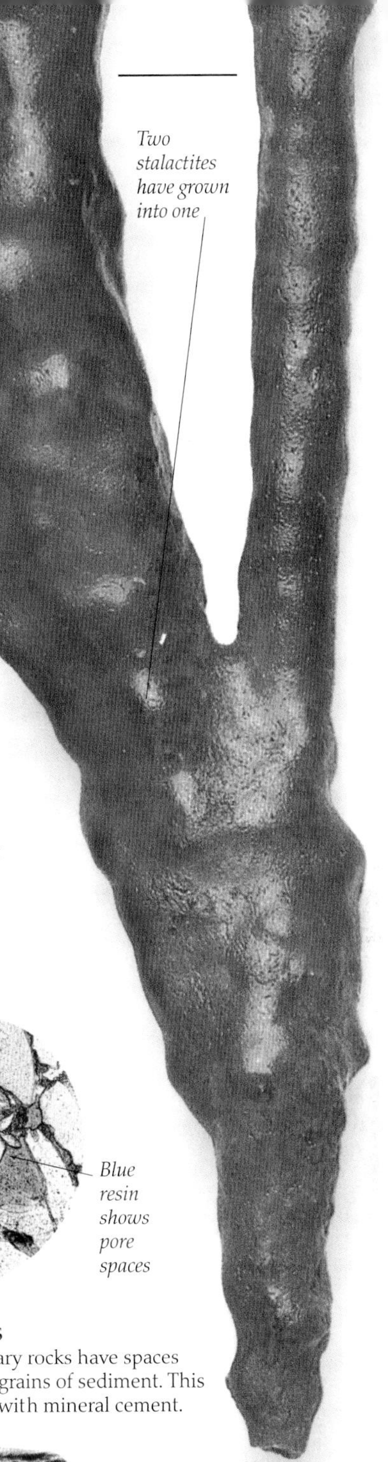

Two stalactites have grown into one

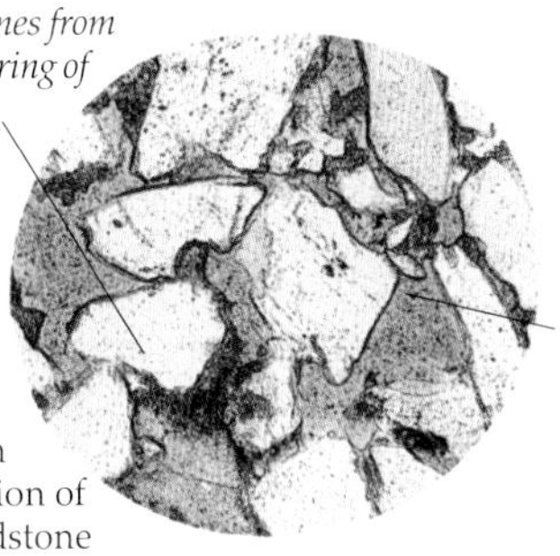

Cement comes from the weathering of other rocks
Blue resin shows pore spaces

Thin section of sandstone

PORE SPACES

All sedimentary rocks have spaces between the grains of sediment. This may later fill with mineral cement.

Life from rock

ROCKS WEATHER AT THE SURFACE of the Earth, where they come into contact with moist air. As soon as plants take root in the weathered saprolite (p. 50), the process of making soil begins. Factors that govern how soil is formed include climate, vegetation, topography, and the nature of the rock from which the soil is made. In addition to the mineral material from rock, soil also contains organic material, known as humus. This includes plant roots, decaying plant and animal matter, microorganisms, and the organic chemicals that are part of the decomposition of plant and animal matter as fungi and microbes break it down. Animals, including snails and worms, are part of the organic matter. Water and air between the particles are a vital part of soil; without them, plants would suffocate or dehydrate. The natural processes that make soil are slow and complex, taking tens of thousands of years. By contrast, soil can be used up rapidly, becoming depleted within as little as a decade.

EARTH MOTHER
In early agricultural civilizations, the fertility of women and the fertility of the soil were seen as two parts of the miraculous continuity of life. In ancient Roman mythology, Proserpina, the daughter of Ceres, the Roman goddess of fruitfulness, was abducted into the underworld, where she ate some pomegranate seeds. During the months she was imprisoned, the crops would not grow, animals were no longer fertile, and death stalked the land—the months of winter.

TERRACING FOR AGRICULTURE
Artificial terraces, where the hillside is cut into steps, make the slopes easier to farm. They provide land that is level and more convenient to irrigate and plow. Terraces have the added advantage of stabilizing slopes by reducing the rate at which soil is lost from the slope to the valley below. Terracing is commonly found with rice cultivation.

Terraced slopes in Yemen

Terraced slope

Podzolic soil (found in temperate climates)

A-horizon contains organic matter

B-horizon has little organic matter

C-horizon is the rock layer

SOIL PROFILE
A section dug through soil down to the underlying rock reveals the soil profile. It has a number of distinct layers. The top layer is called the A-horizon. Within this layer, the gardener or farmer digs or plows through the topsoil. Below lies the B-horizon, which may contain accumulations of mineral matter washed in from the upper layers. The B-horizon has more rock fragments from the underlying parent rock. The C-horizon contains a large percentage of broken and weathered rock from which the overlying soil has been derived.

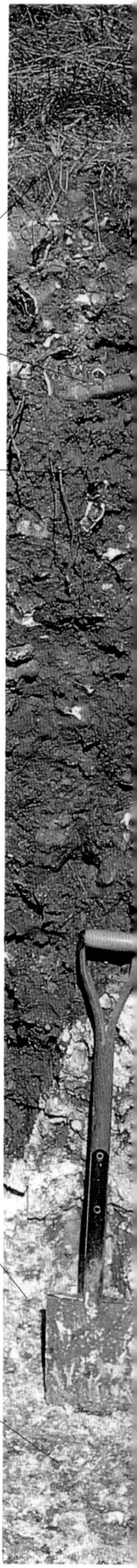

Brown soil (high humus content)

A-horizon contains organic matter

Chalk weathered away, leaving flint behind

B-horizon has little organic matter

C-horizon is the rock layer

Chalk

., AIR, AND WATER
way soil particles lump together
nportant to cultivation. So is the
of the mineral grains. Clay soils
abundant moisture and
ients, but water passes
ugh slowly. Plants
it difficult to gain root
and extract nutrients.
dy soils have large pore
es and water washes
ugh, so they are
ively poor in nutrients.
nvestigate the nature
e two soils, the same
ght of each soil is
ed in a test tube and a
sured amount of water
dded. The difference in
r penetration can be
ly seen. The ideal
lies somewhere
veen the two.

Water is quickly absorbed in the air spaces
Water is slow to drain
Sandy soil
Clay soil
Sandy soil
Clay soil

SOIL CREEP
Soil is constantly on the move downhill because of the influence of gravity. Animals walking across a slope also gently nudge the soil as they go. When it rains, soil becomes wet and may move as a mud flow. When soil freezes, soil particles move out from the slope. After thawing, these particles settle lower down the slope. Trees on a hillside often show this movement of the soil. As young saplings, they grow vertically. Gradually, the soil creep tips them down the slope, until they stick out at an angle. The tree sometimes grows in a curve as it tries to maintain its vertical growth upward into the light.

VING ORGANISM
is the interface between life and the rocky part
e Earth. Without it, life would be impossible.
in the soil that chemical exchanges take
e that allow plants to grow. When plants
they give back their chemical content to
soil. Microorganisms in the soil (fungi
bacteria) convert dead plant and
nal matter into simpler
micals that enrich the soil.
arvesting a crop, some
he fertility of the soil
ken away. If the
is to continue
roduce crops,
ust regain
ients from
weathering,
om added
lizers.

Wildflowers
Grass
Snail
Decomposing leaf
Dark humus-rich soil
lug
Animal burrow
Pebbles
Roots

Erosion

WATER FALLING
As rivers cut their pathway from the mountains down to sea level, irregularities in the rocks or any change in the pathway can make rapids, a waterfall, or a lake. Waterfalls mark a place in the river's pathway where active erosion is taking place. Waterfalls are also common in valleys that have been glaciated (pp. 58–59).

WEATHERING BREAKS DOWN ROCKS to form loose material or rock minerals in solution. Erosion is all the ways in which the material in solution and the loose rock fragments are removed from the location of the original rock and transported to another place, usually under the influence of gravity. Rock material may be carried by water, it may be transported by glacier ice (pp. 58–59), or it may be blown by the wind. The amount of rock fragments carried relates to the speed at which water is traveling, so fast-moving rivers can erode huge amounts of landscape during a flood. During erosion and transportation, the rock fragments are sorted according to their size and density. The chemical elements that went into solution may travel as far as the ocean, where they make the ocean more salty. In temperate climates, where it rains often, clay and sand grains are carried away by rainwater washing over slopes, and then by rivers. The heaviest rock fragments are dropped first wherever the speed of the river slackens. At coastlines where cliffs meet the sea, the land is continually being eroded.

IRREGULAR COASTLINE
Waves beating on a shore hit headlands first. As they meet shallower water, the waves curve around and then break against the sides of the headland. If there are joint planes (p. 51) in the rock, or softer rocks, these are eroded away more rapidly than the hard headland rocks. First, an archway forms. Then, if the roof of the arch caves in, an isolated sea stack is left. Waves that hit the coast at an angle move rock fragments along the shore sideways.

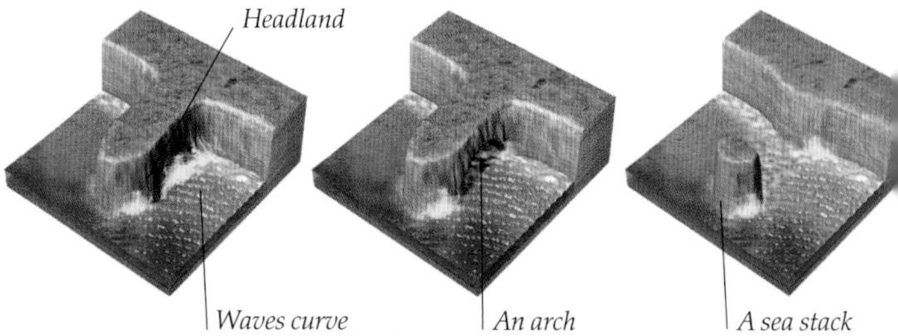

Headland
Waves curve around headland
An arch forms
A sea stack results

Wave fronts curve

Man O'War cove, southern Britain

WAVES AS AGENTS OF EROSION
Waves are formed by winds blowing over water. The wave fronts in deep water are parallel to one another. As they meet shallower water, they bend and hit the shore in a curve. These curved waves affect the shape of the shoreline. The offshore reef on this coastline breaks up the wave energy. The resulting curved wavelets contribute to the characteristic shape of the cove. Each incoming wave moves pebbles and sand along the beach sideways; the backflowing water moves the material back down the beach.

CHANGING CLIFF FACE
Waves that meet a steep rocky shore directly break with all their force against the foot of the cliff. Here, solution and weathering happen as salty water continually wets the rock and then dries out at low tide. Salt crystallization occurs and breaks up the grains of the rock. The cliffs are undercut, primarily by wave action, and eventually the upper part falls, breaking along a crack that may be an original joint plane in the rock. The shape of the cliff depends on the resistance of the different rocks to the pounding of the waves.

Arch
Headland
Sea stack

Normandy cliffs, France

sive
bed has
ted erosion
Area of rock
has eroded
more easily

SALT CRYSTALLIZATION

Pinnacles of rock weathered in a dry climate show hard bands of rock that stand out on the surface. Other layers are more easily weathered and eroded. This uneven sculpting by the weather relates to the changes in grain size and pore size from one rock layer to another. Large pore sizes allow water to penetrate deeply into the rock when it rains. In a dry climate, or where there are high winds, the surface dries before the interior of the rock does. Later, as the pore water dries, salts weathered out from the rock crystallize just under the surface. These push apart the rock grains. The loosened grains are blown away by the wind.

Sand dune in Morocco

SANDS OF TIME

Weathering in the desert is a result of fracturing brought about by temperature changes and by salt crystallization. Erosion is mostly caused by the wind, which always blows away the smallest particles and flaky mineral grains, leaving rounded quartz sand. These sand grains are transported across the surface of the desert, where they form sand dunes. The dunes also move, with sand being blown up the gentle slope and sliding in occasional avalanches down the steep slope.

Wadi
Slopes are covered with weathering rock fragments
Natural rock arch
Sand dunes
Rock fragments collect in wadi

MODEL OF A DESERT LANDSCAPE

The notion of deserts as only sandy places is not accurate. Antarctica (p. 18) is a desert because, like the Sahara, it receives less than 10 in (25 cm) of rainfall each year. When torrential rain does come to arid areas, whole mountainsides may be swept clean of boulders, rock fragments, sand, and clay in flash floods that pour down wadis (dry river valleys) to drain into temporary lakes, or playas. The rock fragments building up in gullies at the foot of steep mountainsides may be weathered to make sand. The sand is washed out, or blown away to form dunes.

HOLES IN THE RIVERBED

Sometimes rivers disappear underground in caves known as sinkholes. Some of these are enlarged cracks in limestone, but others are formed by the collapse of the limestone over an underground cave. Limestone weathers and erodes into cave systems if the rock is hard enough to be self-supporting when it is hollowed out. The best limestones for this are fine-grained limy muds (p. 51) that have been cemented together to make a tough rock. More shelly limestones form cave systems less readily.

Deposition

ALL THE ROCK FRAGMENTS broken off from the solid rocky surface of the Earth are deposited somewhere else as sediment. The environment of deposition varies enormously, and this controls the character of the sediment. If the circumstances are just right, the sediments may eventually become new sedimentary rocks. The environments of deposition vary from steep mountain slopes to flat river valleys, to beaches to the seabed on the continental shelf, and to the deep ocean floor. Many sediments that are laid down are eroded again fairly soon afterward. This might happen as pebbles are dropped after a river floods and then picked up and transported farther downstream in the next flood. During this time, the pebbles and other grains undergo weathering and are transported farther. The best place for sediments to be made into rock is a location where the land surface is sinking, or where the sea level is rising. Under these circumstances, one sediment layer is rapidly buried by another and is preserved. Once buried, it becomes compressed and hardened to make rock.

Vale of Glamorgan coast, Wales

SHAPING THE BE
Coastal beaches are places of continual change (p.
The nature of the waves breaking on this beach causes
banks of pebbles to be scoured and sorted. However, e
beaches have definite seasonal cycles. Sand moves o
the beach in summer, while in winter the high w
usually pick the sand up and deposit it offsh

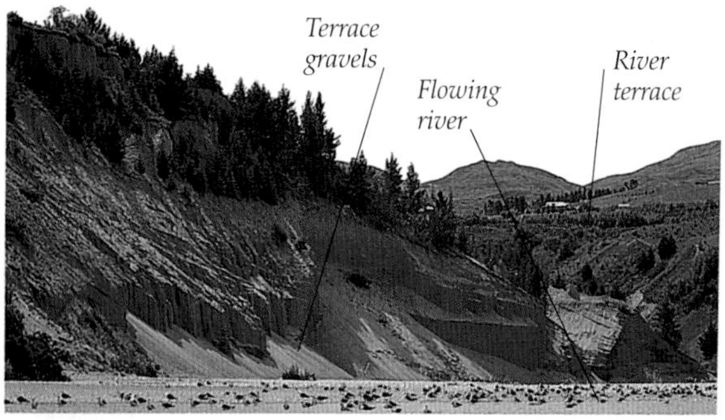

Terrace gravels
Flowing river
River terrace

Shotover River, New Zealand

RIVER TERRACES
When a river falls in response to a drop in sea level, the level of the old flood plain is abandoned above the flowing river. These new incised banks are known as terraces. The terraces are made of older sands and gravel that were previously part of the riverbed.

MEANDERING RIVER
The flatter parts of river valleys are where the river drops the load of sediment it has collected from the fast-flowing hilly portion of its pathway. Meandering river valleys are sometimes flat and wide. The river moves in snakelike fashion, the course changing with every flood to make great loops. If the river cuts through the neck of the loop, the abandoned loop is known as an ox-bow lake.

Mara River, Tanzania

Erosion on the outside of the curve
Deposition of sediment on the inside of the curve
Neck of loop

RIVERS OF SAND
Erosion dominates in the steep parts of the river and deposition in the flood plain area. The river erodes its banks on the outside of a bend, where the flow is fastest, and the sediment is redeposited on the insides of bends, where the flow is slow. Meandering rivers build wide flat valleys, called flood plains, made from their deposited material, as shown in this model.

BUILDING A DELTA
Sediments are deposited wherever the velocity of the river water lessens. If this happens where a river flows into the sea or a lake, it builds a delta which slowly makes more land. This satellite photograph shows how sand, silt, and river mud are being deposited at the mouths of the Ganges and Brahmaputra rivers in the Bay of Bengal. The shape of the delta and the rate of land building depend on many factors, especially the rate of subsidence of the delta region.

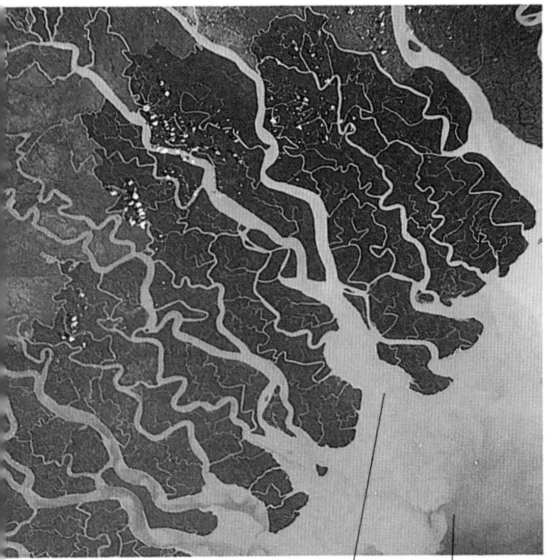

ges-Brahmaputra Delta
River mouth
Bay of Bengal

FORMATION OF ESTUARINE MUD
River water flows to the tidal estuary and suddenly becomes muddy. This happens because salty water causes the tiny clay particles suspended in fresh river water to clump together into larger particles. While the single clay flakes were small enough to remain in suspension, the clumps are too large, so they sink to the riverbed. This increases the amount of sediment and helps to build up river deltas.

Clay in salty water
Clay in freshwater
In freshwater, clay particles remain in suspension
In salty water, clay particles clump together and are deposited more quickly

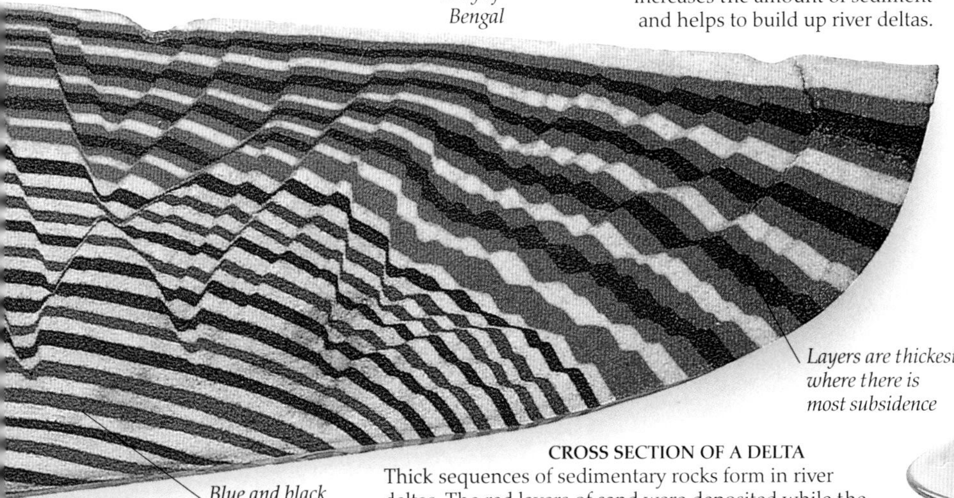

Layers are thickest where there is most subsidence
Blue and black layers represent older rocks laid down before stretching

CROSS SECTION OF A DELTA
Thick sequences of sedimentary rocks form in river deltas. The red layers of sand were deposited while the model was stretched (p. 47), and the layers are thickest where there is most subsidence. These deltas may be places where oil accumulated (p. 27).

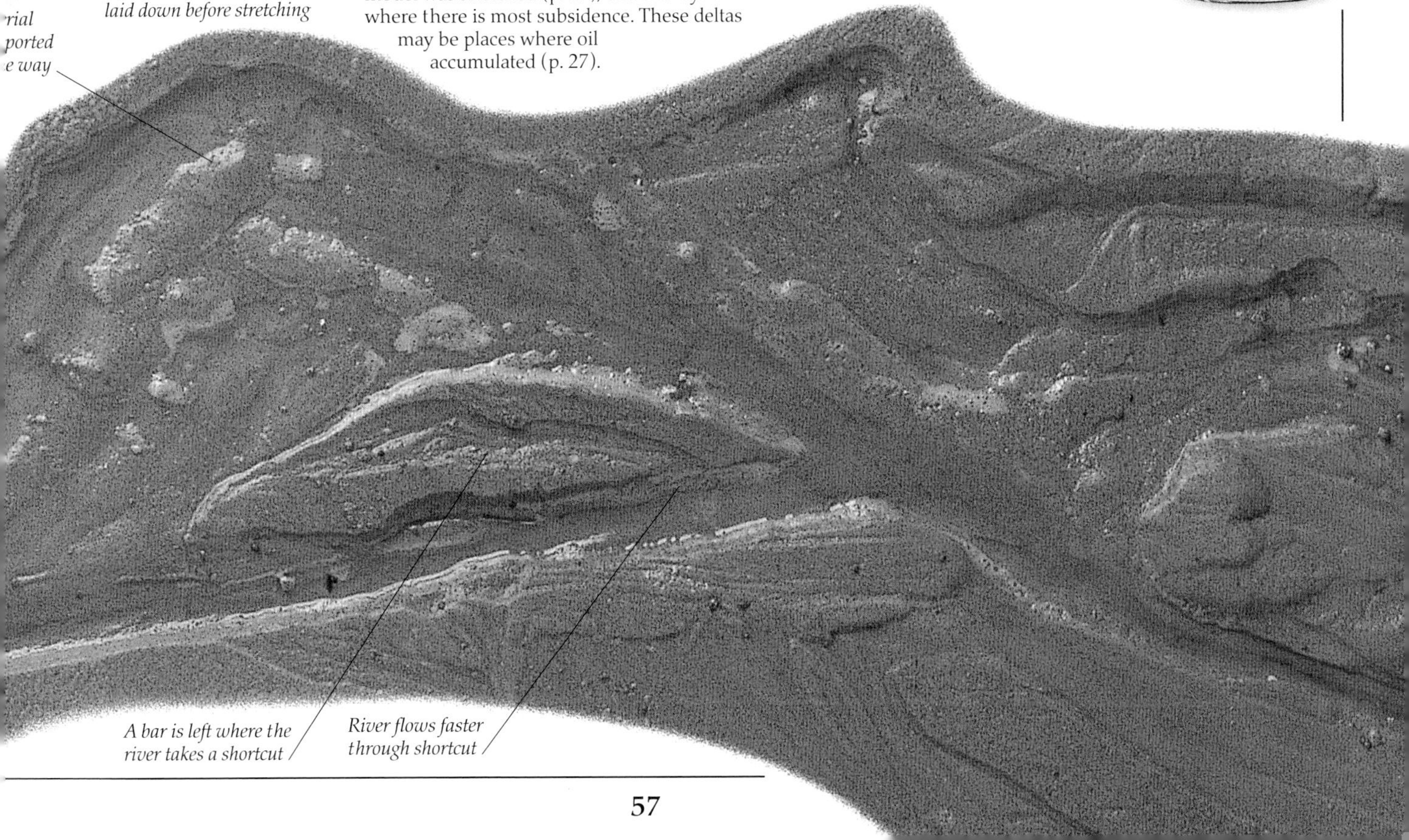

rial
ported
e way
A bar is left where the river takes a shortcut
River flows faster through shortcut

Glaciation

GLACIERS ARE FOUND IN THE HIGH VALLEYS of many mountain ranges today, although most are melting faster than they are being replenished by snowfall, which explains why the valley end of the glacier is retreating higher up the mountain. Today's mountain glaciers are but a small leftover from the great glaciers that filled the valleys in the cold stages of the Pleistocene Ice Age. Ten thousand years ago glaciers started to melt faster than they were supplied with snow. It must have taken the same sort of time for the glaciers to build up. Over the last two million years, glacier buildup has happened each time a cold, wet, glacial period followed a warmer, interglacial period. The Earth today is thought to be in an interglacial period of glacier melting. As valley glaciers flow, they carve their valleys wider and deeper, eventually making a U-shaped trough. Melting glaciers are hemmed in by mounds of sediments that were washed out of the ice. These fragments have been plucked from the surrounding rocks and transported downhill by the glaciers as they move down the valleys. In this way glaciers can transport huge amounts of rock fragments from mountain summits to valley floors.

SATELLITE SNOWSCAPE
Alaska, Canada, much of the northern US and Scandinavia, as well as Antarctica and Greenland, were ice-covered at the coldes stages of the Pleistocene Ice Age. Today, so of these regions are still snow-covered in wi while only their mountainous regions hav permanent glacier ice. In winter, as seen i Alaska from satellite, pack-ice builds up aro the coast as the water freezes and the first wi snow falls. In Siberia, Alaska, and norther Canada, great regions still have permanent frozen ground known as permafrost, although this is reducing in area.

GLACIER GIANTS
Where a glacier melts at its snout, a water torrent may flow from the bouldery gravel mounds left by the melting ice. The gravel heaps are known as the terminal moraine of the glacier. The great rivers of Europe, such as the Rhine, all have their source in the melting glaciers of the Alps. Here we see the Bridge River Glacier in British Columbia, Canada.

MELTING ICE
At present, a high rate of global warming is resulting in the melting of glaciers and polar ice. This may lead to a rise in sea levels, flooding low-lying areas. Evidence can be seen in the crumbling blocks calving off the Neumayer Glacier (left) in South Georgia.

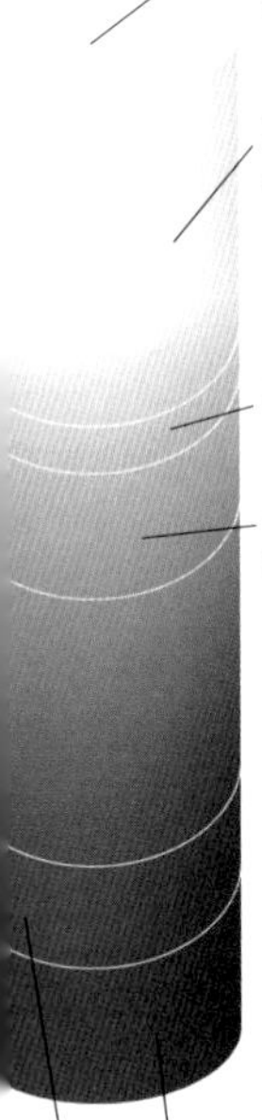

Freshly fallen snow
New snow
Névé
Glacier ice
Air
ezed out
Impermeable ice

GRAY ICE

During the summer, the mature snow on top of glacier ice melts. Dust, either volcanic or blown rock dust, becomes concentrated on the melted surface as a dark veneer (right). The gray snow surface absorbs the Sun's radiation and speeds up summer melting. The winter snowfalls make a new white layer, and in this way dark dust layers mark each summer melt in glacier ice.

FROM SNOW TO ICE

Falling snow is made of fluffy flakes that trap air in the new snowfall layer. As the fluffy snow warms and partly melts in daytime and refreezes at night, the crystals grow more compact, with less air between. This more mature snow is called névé. Eventually, what used to be light airy snow is compacted into solid hard ice.

French Alps, near Chamonix

CREATING FIORDS

Glaciers flow slowly and do not easily go around corners, as rivers do. Most grow in existing river valleys, and their flow erodes the sides and floor of the valley. After the glacier melts, what was once a V-shaped meandering river valley has become a straight, U-shaped trough. In mountainous areas near a coastline, the sea floods into the valleys, many of which are below the new global sea level that rose as the glaciers melted. Many coastal inlets formed in this way off the west coast of Norway, and so they are known by the Norwegian name, *fjord*. Fiords are also found around the northern continents and in Antarctica and New Zealand.

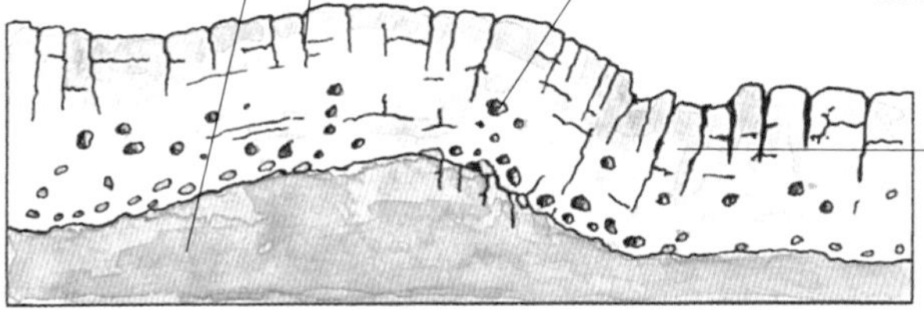

Bedrock
Glacier ice
Plucked boulder
Meltwater seeps into cracks

PLUCKED ROCK

As the glacier passes over a block of rock, some ice melts and trickles into cracks in the rock, where it freezes again. This uses the rock to be plucked off the solid ey floor and carried along by the glacier.

GLACIER GRATER

The rocky floor over which glacier ice and boulders travel becomes polished by the rock fragments trapped in the flowing glacier. The smoothed surface shows scratches (striae) on the surface (left). The glacier transports the fine rock powder that each scratch makes. This powder, along with all the rock fragments, contributes to the glacier's total rock load. The unsorted mass of fine rock powder and small and large rock fragments is left in heaps wherever the glacier melts.This rock is called boulder clay (right), which makes a hummocky landscape.

Boulder clay cemented with lime

Chalky boulder clay

NTINENTAL ICE SHEET

interiors of Greenland and Antarctica are covered with ice sheets thousands eet thick. The thickness reduces toward the edge of the landmass. Near the st of northwest Greenland, valley glaciers are threading their way through untains that ring the island. Rock fragments are carried along the edges of the ier (lateral moraines), and also within the ice itself.

The age of the Earth

JAMES USSHER (1581–1656)
This 17th-century clergyman used biblical evidence to show that the Earth was created in 4004 BCE. He based his calculation on the genealogies in the Bible. Ussher's date was believed by many scientists and the general public for a time. Other religions came up with a date for the beginning of the Earth based on their beliefs.

WHEN THINKING ABOUT HOW OLD the Earth might be, James Hutton (p. 8) wrote in 1788 that he could see "no vestige of a beginning, no prospect of an end." Hutton saw geological time as being unimaginably long. It was not until the 20th century, with the understanding of radioactivity, that an accurate method of dating such old materials as Earth rocks was developed. This was radiometric dating that used a measurable Earth process that happened on a time scale of the right order of magnitude. Another method of dating rocks and therefore the age of the Earth is to study layers in sedimentary rocks, and fossils—dead plants and animals that have become preserved in rocks of the Earth's crust. This record in the rocks also helps to reveal past climates, giving information about how the atmosphere used to be on the Earth. The ocean floor preserves the Earth's magnetic field, making a record that goes back 200 million years.

WILLIAM THOMSON (1824–1907)
This British scientist (later Lord Kel
calculated the age of the Earth base
on the length of time it had taken t
cool to its present temperature. He
assumed that the Earth originally h
a molten surface. The time he came
with was 40 million years. This was
too short to account for the evoluti
of life or for the accumulation of
sedimentary rock strata (p. 62).

TIME GAPS
The thickness of rock layers might look like a good way to date Earth processes, but the rates of sedimentation are difficult to measure. One problem is that the layers contain many time gaps when no strata were laid down or they were eroded. Some gaps represent a very long time interval. From fossils and radiometric dating, the time interval represented at this rock outcrop in southern Britain is 160 million years: the time between when the lower set of rocks was being laid down as sediments to when it was submerged and buried by new layers of rocks. Such a time gap between deposition of rock layers is called an unconformity.

USING FOSSILS
The British geologist Charles Lyell (p. 62) realized that young rocks contain many fossils that are similar to living life forms, and that progressively older rocks have fewer and fewer species that resemble modern forms. Palaeontologists who study fossils and stratigraphers who study rock sequences, have compiled an Earth history that allows rocks to be dated from their fossils. For example, *Acadagnostus* is found in Middle Cambrian rocks, while *Eocyphinium* is found in rocks of Carboniferous age.

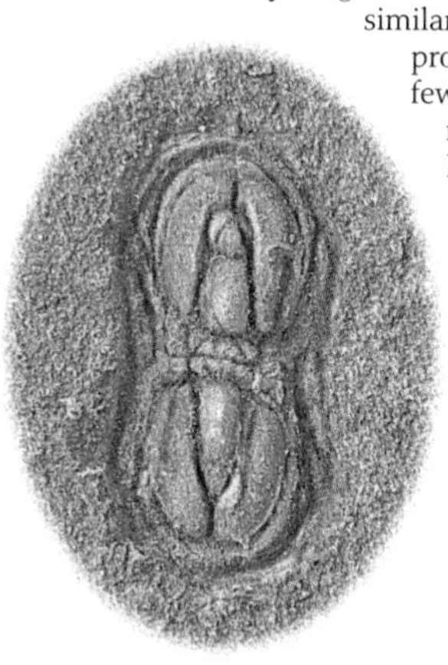

Acadagnostus

Eocyphinium

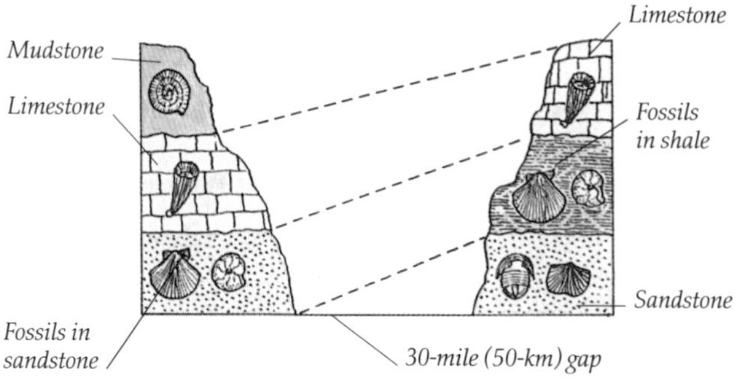
Mudstone
Limestone
Fossils in sandstone
Limestone
Fossils in shale
Sandstone
30-mile (50-km) gap

CORRELATING WITH FOSSILS
Fossils can be used to match rocks from one
place to another. Correlation assumes two
things—that evolution of all members of a
species took place at the same time worldw
and that evolution never reproduces a speci
once it has become extinct. The fossils of
creatures that died and were buried at the
same time sometimes appear in different ro
types. Two rocks, such as sandstone and sha
can be formed at the same time, perhaps
where a sandy beach changed along the
coastline into a muddy estuary.

sing
ing
netic
le
Mirror to show movement of needle
Marble cylinder holds a pair of coils to produce a magnetic field
eral
ple
ed here

Marble plinth to isolate the magnet

MAGNETOMETER
Carefully orientated specimens of lava can be collected and taken back to the laboratory. When placed within the magnetic field of a magnetometer, the direction of their magnetic alignment can be determined. This gives a clue to the age of the lava.

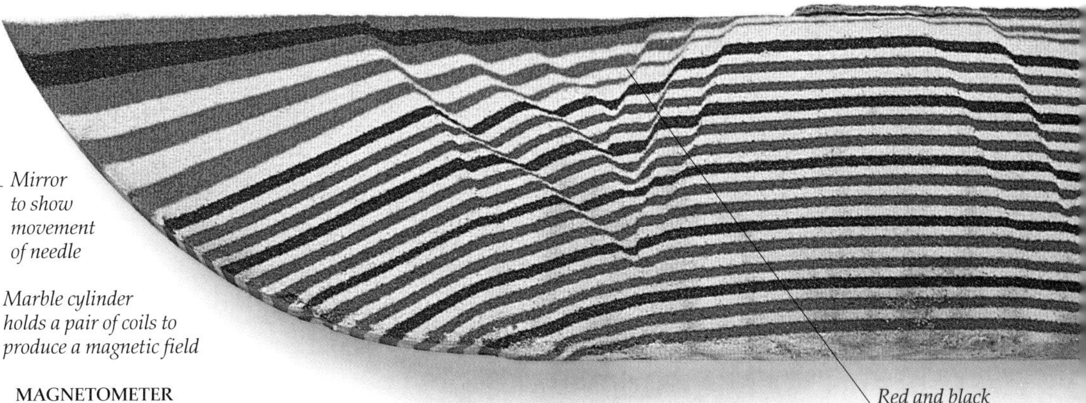

Red and black layers are sediments

Laboratory model of a sedimentary basin

STRATIGRAPHY—HISTORY THROUGH MAGNETISM
Sedimentary rocks contain grains of magnetic minerals that are weathered from preexisting igneous rocks. As these grains come to rest in a heap of sediments, each grain orientates itself, like a compass needle, with the Earth's magnetic field (p. 6). So a sequence of sedimentary rocks can be correlated with normal and reversed polarity (p. 39) and compared with their radiometric dates. Some rock types are more suitable than others; red sandstones and shales are particularly useful because they are rich in iron.

E RINGS
age of a felled tree can be calculated by the growth
s in the trunk. Each year is characterized by its
particular growth ring. The oldest trees on
Earth, such as the North American
le-cone pines, allow these records
e taken back thousands of
s. With this information,
ated wood, such as that
ilized within recent
flows, can be
rately dated.

wth
s
ng layers
ood on
outside
he trunk

Fossilized tree trunk

Amino acids are extracted from bone for radiocarbon dating

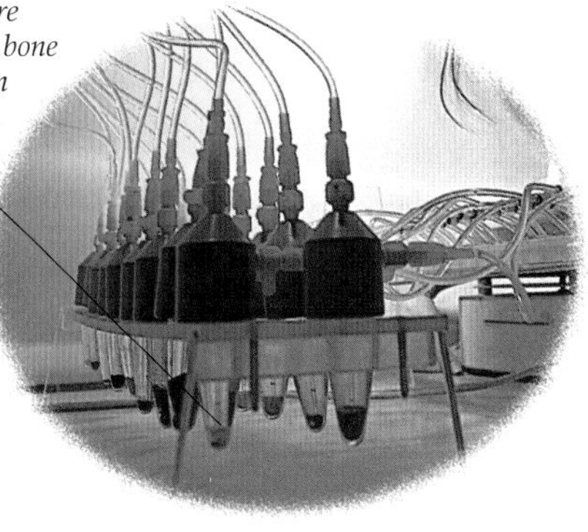

RADIOMETRIC DATING
This dating method works from measuring the rate of transformation of one radioactive isotope (parent) to its daughter element. Some radioactive parent/daughter transformations take longer than the age of the Earth. These long-life radioactive elements, such as uranium, are used to date the oldest rocks.

IN THE LABORATORY
Once an organism dies, its carbon content is no longer being renewed. Radiocarbon dating measures how much carbon 14 is left in a dead organism in relation to carbon 12. In 5,570 years, half of all the carbon 14 in a sample will have changed to carbon 12. This short half-life means that carbon 14 is only suitable for dating wood, bone, and young rocks—those from the last 70,000 years. In this laboratory, a mass spectrometer is being used to sort and count the amounts of each isotope.

Naming the Earth

THE MOST RECENT HISTORY of the Earth is the best known, because the younger rocks contain abundant fossils and there is a fairly complete rock record. We know much less about the first 3 billion years because the rocks contain few and only primitive fossils, and many of the rocks have been metamorphosed several times. Also, much of the rock record is either buried by younger rocks or has been eroded to make sedimentary rocks.

CHARLES LYELL (1797–1875)
Lyell's most fundamental contribution to geology was his belief in Uniformitarianism, that "the present is the key to the pas It is now known that this is a decidedly limited truth, as Precambrian history shows. A Earth processes—plate tectoni mountain building, weatherin sedimentation—had a beginni probably early in the Precambrian.

AGE OF THE EARTH
The Earth is believed to be about 4.5 billion years old. This is supported by the age of the oldest rocks on the Moon, and by dating meteorites, which suggests that our solar system itself may be about this old. Precambrian time includes major events like the origin of the first life-forms, the growth of the continents, the beginnings of plate tectonics, and the buildup of atmospheric oxygen.

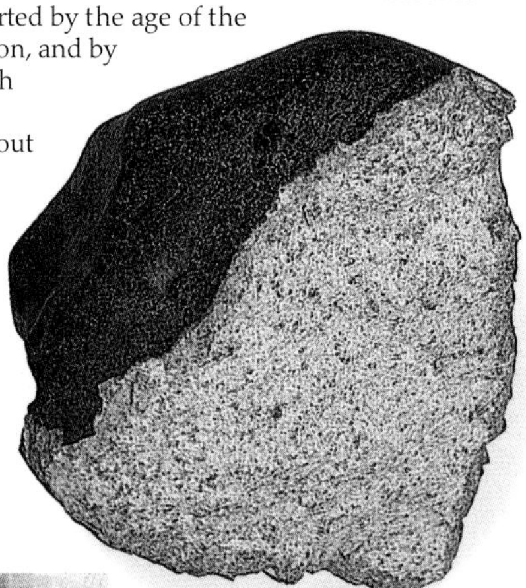

Stony meteorite

Paradoxides

Mastop

SEA SCAVENGERS
The Cambrian marks the time when life became abundant in the oceans and left a clear fossil record of its presence. Trilobites, such as this *Paradoxides*, were bottom-dwellers in shallow seas where they scavenged for food.

OXYGEN GI
Green algaelike *Mastopora* pro oxygen in their metabolism were responsible for relea oxygen into the atmosphere (p.

Goniophyllum

OLD-LIFE CORALS
Corals like *Goniophyllum* are life-forms that are still familiar.

THE PRECAMBRIAN SHIELD
Sir William Logan (p. 41) realized the Precambrian rocks he mapped in the Canadian Shield were enormously old. He called the peculiar structures in these rocks cryptozooans, meaning hidden animal, because these rocks were thought to predate the existence of life.

OLD ROCK
Much of the first solid crust on Earth was probably like basalt in composition and similar to today's ocean floor. The first granites that make the continents must have come later. Today, Precambrian granites have been metamorphosed, perhaps many times over.

Granite gneiss

Collenia

EARLY LIFE
Collenia are stromatolites—blue-green algae that are one of the earliest forms of life. They usually occur in lumpy pillars between high and low tidal water levels.

Pteraspis

BONY F
Some life-forms h an external skelet such as a shell, w others have an inter skeleton. The earl fish lived in the had an exter skeleton of bony pla and were jawless this *Pteras*

ARCHAEAN	PROTEROZOIC	CAMBRIAN	ORDOVICIAN	SILURIAN	DEVONI
PRECAMBRIAN		PALEOZOIC			
4.5 Bya	2.5 Bya	590 Mya	500 Mya		400 M

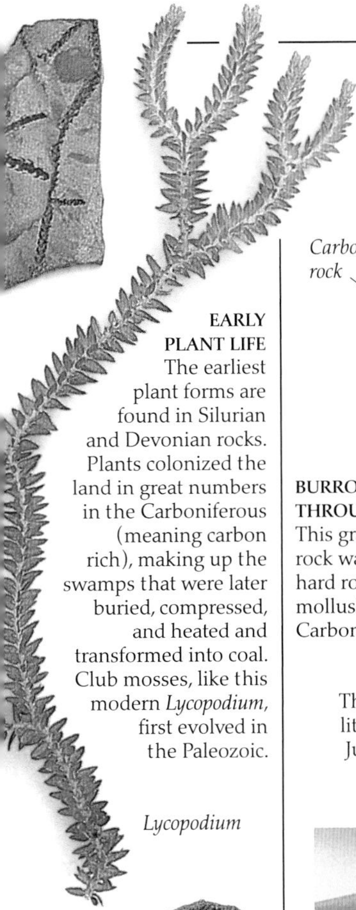

EARLY PLANT LIFE
The earliest plant forms are found in Silurian and Devonian rocks. Plants colonized the land in great numbers in the Carboniferous (meaning carbon rich), making up the swamps that were later buried, compressed, and heated and transformed into coal. Club mosses, like this modern *Lycopodium*, first evolved in the Paleozoic.

Lycopodium

DESERT SANDSTONE
Sandstones of Permian
e in Europe show they were
med in a desert climate. The
nd grains are well-rounded,
ving been blown around by
e wind, and are sometimes
sloping layers (pp. 26–27).

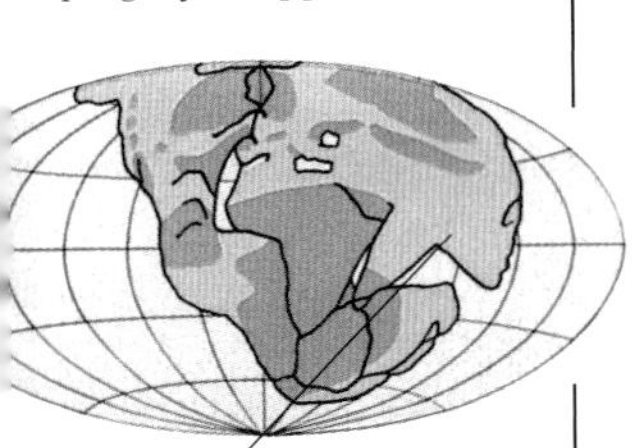

allow seas

RBONIFEROUS MAP
his map of Pangaea, Alfred
gener (pp. 34–35) showed
the continents grouped
gether at the end of
rboniferous times.

Limy sediment formed in the Jurassic sea
Carboniferous rock
Boreholes made by boring mollusk

BURROWS THROUGH TIME
This gray Carboniferous rock was hardened and eroded. It made a hard rocky seabed in Jurassic times. Shelly mollusks in the Jurassic burrowed into the Carboniferous rock.

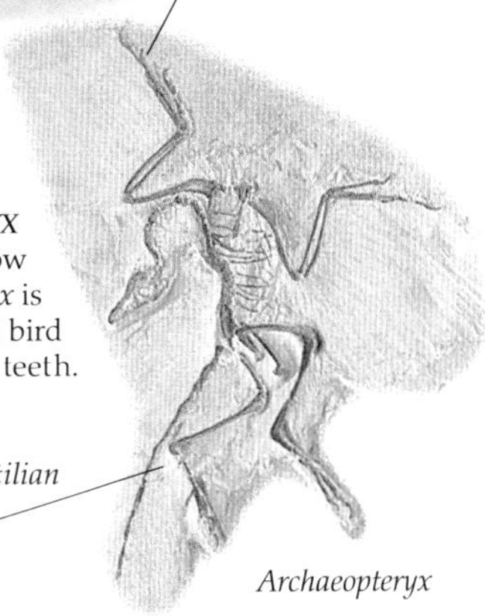

Finger
Reptilian tail

Archaeopteryx

ARCHAEOPTERYX
There are so few fossil birds that we know little about their evolution. *Archaeopteryx* is Jurassic in age and is clearly a feathered bird capable of flying, although it still had teeth.

SANDY DESERT
The deserts of Europe must have been as large as the Gobi Desert of today. Thick deposits of salt indicate temporary lakes which evaporated in the hot climate. The rocks that formed on the shorelines of these lakes sometimes contain footprints or fossilized skeletons of dinosaurs.

EUROPEAN CHALK
The end of the Mesozoic saw extensive seas in which pure limestone was laid down. The Chalk is made of the shells of tiny algae.

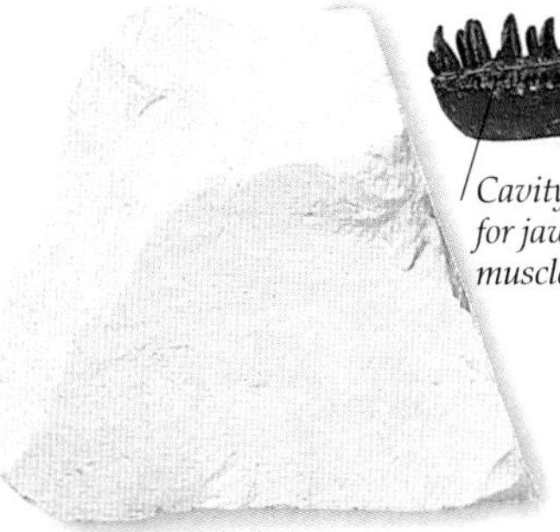

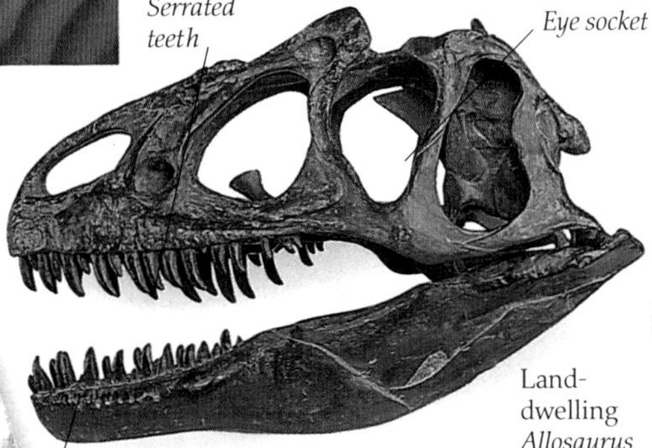

Serrated teeth
Eye socket
Cavity for jaw muscles

Land-dwelling *Allosaurus*

DINOSAUR FOSSILS
Creatures that lived in the water and dropped to the bottom when they died had a better chance of becoming preserved as fossils. The fossil record is dominated by water-dwelling creatures. Land animals like the meat-eating *Allosaurus* were rarely preserved.

THE ROCKY MOUNTAINS
A high mountain chain was built along the subduction zones on the west of the Americas. Today, global topography is much more varied than is usual in the Earth's history, with many high mountain ranges that are actively being lifted up and eroded (pp. 54–55).

THE GREAT ICE AGE
One cause of the Ice Age in the Pleistocene epoch (a subdivision of the Quaternary) may be the high mountains and their locations, which affected global weather systems by diverting surface winds.

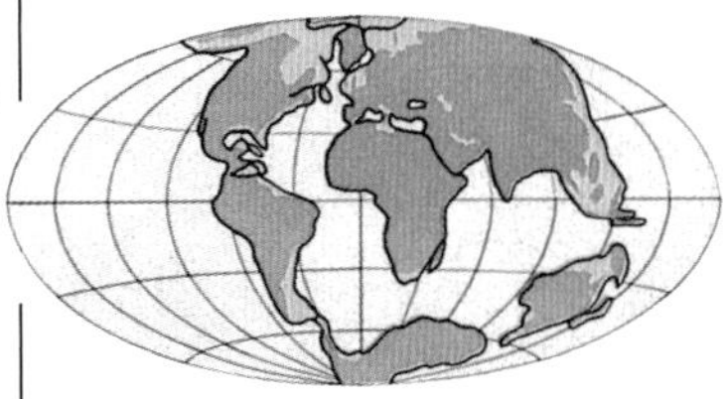

RECENT LANDSCAPE
Alfred Wegener's map for late Tertiary times showed the world much as it is today, although with a narrower North Atlantic Ocean. During Tertiary times, major mountain ranges were built, such as the modern Alps and Himalayas (pp. 46–47).

RBONIFEROUS	**PERMIAN**	**TRIASSIC**	**JURASSIC**	**CRETACEOUS**	**TERTIARY**	**QUATERNARY**
PALEOZOIC		**MESOZOIC**			**CENOZOIC**	
300 Mya		**200 Mya**		**100 Mya**	**65 Mya**	

Did you know?

FASCINATING FACTS

During the 1980 volcanic eruption of Mount St. Helens in Washington state, 520 million tons of searing hot ash were dumped over an area of more than 22,000 square miles (56,980 sq km) in just 9 hours. Towns up to 250 miles (402 km) away were shrouded in complete darkness.

A plume of ash rises above Mount St. Helens in May 1980

Scientists have tracked dust carried by storms from western China to the United States. African dust carried by trade winds has also made its way to Florida.

Equatorial regions are typically thought of as Earth's hot spots, but on Ecuador's Mount Cotopaxi, it's cold enough for a glacier.

Scientists estimate that over the last 500 years volcanoes have claimed the lives of 300,000 people. The countries with the most historically active volcanoes are, in descending order: Indonesia, Japan, and the United States.

The world's deepest lake is Lake Baikal in Siberia. This 20-million-year-old lake contains an astonishing 20 percent of the Earth's fresh liquid water in its 5,712-ft (1,741-m) depths.

Mud is certainly messy, but when it is on the move, it can also be lethal. While most mudslides move at 10–20 mph (16–32 kph), some slides have been clocked at speeds of an astonishing 100 mph (160 kph).

How can scientists study the ocean floor without getting wet? They can go to Iceland, where the Mid-Atlantic Ridge rises above sea level and where the same processes that create the seafloor are visible on dry land.

Some icebergs floating in the freezing seas of Antarctica are mammoth in size. In 2003, an iceberg was measured at 125 miles (200 km) long and more than 19 miles (30.5 km) wide—that's twice the size of the state of Rhode Island.

View of Lake Baikal

If a highway could be built straight up from Earth to space you could drive there in about an hour!

During any given minute of any day about a thousand thunderstorms occur on Earth. These produce about a hundred lightning strikes a second!

There's a whole lot of shaking going on in California. The average rate of motion across its San Andreas Fault Zone is about 2 in (5 cm) per year, about the same rate as your fingernails grow. If this continues, seismologists predict that Los Angeles and San Francisco will be right next to each other in approximately 15 million years.

The smallest part of an iceberg floats above water

These icebergs have broken from glaciers in Paradise Bay, Antarctica

Damage from a California earthquake

QUESTIONS AND ANSWERS

Q What elements make up the Earth's rocks?

A Although there is a huge variety of rock found on Earth, most rocks consist of just eight elements: oxygen, silicon, aluminum, iron, calcium, magnesium, potassium, and sodium.

Q How much of the Earth's surface is volcanic rock?

A About three-quarters of the rocks on the Earth's surface are volcanic in origin. Most of the rocks found on the seafloor were created by volcanoes.

Diamond

Q What is the largest diamond ever found?

A The Cullinan, a 3,106-carat diamond, was found in 1905 in South Africa. It was cut into smaller gems, among them the legendary Great Star of Africa, part of England's Crown Jewels.

Q Approximately how much gold has been found to date?

A So far, 425,000,000 lb (192,776,757 kg) of gold have been mined from the Earth. That's about enough to build a seven-story building.

Q How old are the Earth's rocks?

A Rocks on the continents have been dated at a staggering 4.5 billion years old. The rocks on the ocean floor are comparatively young, at 300 million years old.

Q How many minerals are there on Earth?

A There are around 4,000 minerals known to exist.

Q What is the hardest mineral? The softest? The most common?

A Talc (used to make talcum powder) is the softest known mineral, and diamond is the hardest. Feldspar is the most common mineral found in the Earth's crust.

Q What are gemstones? What gives them their beautiful colors?

A Gemstones are mineral crystals with a chemistry and structure that make them look special. Only 16 minerals yield important gemstones. Impurities (elements not present in the mineral's pure compound) are what give color to gemstones.

Q What is the largest gold nugget?

A The largest gold nugget known to exist today is the 61-lb (27.6-kg) nugget named the Hand of Faith. It is on display at the Golden Nugget Casino in Las Vegas, Nevada.

The rocks on the ocean floor are much younger than the rocks that make up the Earth's surface

Record Breakers

- **DEATH VALLEY**
  This California desert is one of the hottest places on Earth, with temperatures measuring up to 134°F (56.6°C).
- **MT. EVEREST**
  At 29,035 ft (8,850 m), this Himalayan Mountain peak is the tallest on Earth.
- **NILE RIVER**
  Africa's Nile winds its way on a 4,160-mile- (6,694-km-) long path.
- **MARIANA TRENCH**
  The deepest spot in the ocean is at the bottom of this Pacific trench: at 36,190 ft (11,031 m), it is nearly 7 miles (11 km) deep.
- **MAUNA LOA**
  This Hawaiian volcano is the tallest on Earth, with its cone 50,000 ft (15,240 m) above its base.
- **CASPIAN SEA**
  The largest lake in the world by surface area and volume is Europe's Caspian Sea, with an area of some 144,000 sq miles (372,958 sq km).
- **SAHARA DESERT**
  The largest desert on Earth, Africa's Sahara covers an area about the same size as the United States.

Sahara Desert

Geoscientists at work

How do we know what we know about the planet Earth? Its inner workings are revealed through the Earth sciences, also known as geoscience. Geoscientists study every part of our home planet, from the outermost reaches of the atmosphere to the innermost core at the center of the Earth. These scientists use physics, mathematics, chemistry, and biology—as well as hammers, snorkels, computers, and microscopes—to help us understand the complete life story of our life-giving planet. They gather and interpret data from the Earth's long history to help predict its future. Their work varies widely because the geosciences are so diverse, but here is an introduction to who's who in the geoscientific world.

Geology

A geologist gathers data in the field

Much of the Earth's history is recorded in its rocks; the scientists who study rocks to reveal it are called geologists. Physical geologists study the composition of rocks and the effects of the forces that act upon them. Historical geologists deal with the development of the Earth as evidenced in its rocks. But no matter what their specific focus, all geologists study the Earth. Here are some of the major areas of study within the realm of geology.

Economic geologists explore for locate mineral deposits, and find safe ways to dispose of waste materials from mining. These geologists are often employed by the petrochemical industry or environmental protection groups.

Engineering geologists apply geological data to the study of rocks and soil. They use this information to investigate factors that might affect structures such as bridges, buildings, airports, and dams.

Environmental geologists study the interaction of the Earth—its geosphere, hydrosphere, atmosphere, and biosphere—and human activities. They work to solve issues involving pollution, waste disposal, and urbanization. Environmental scientists also study natural hazards, such as flooding and erosion.

Geochemists use chemistry to investigate the nature and location of elements in groundwater, rock, and soil. They also study the composition of fossil fuel (coal, oil, and gas) deposits.

Geomorphologists study the various landforms and landscapes on Earth in relation to the processes that shaped them. These processes include human activity as well as geological and climatic forces.

Glaciologists (or glacial geologists) study the physical properties and movements of the Earth's glaciers and ice sheets.

Hydrologists study the water cycle, from the moment of precipitation until water evaporates back into the atmosphere or runs into the oceans. A hydrologist might study river systems to predict which areas are at risk in a flood.

Mineralogists study the formation, composition, and properties of Earth's minerals.

Paleontologists use fossils to understand past life-forms and how they changed. They also use fossil evidence to determine what life was like in the Earth's past.

Petroleum geologists are involved in the location and production of oil and natural gas.

Petrologists determine the origin and natural history of rocks by analyzing their composition and studying their grain.

Sedimentologists examine the Earth's sediments (sand, silt, and mud). They study the nature, origin, and distribution of these sediments. Oil, gas, coal, and mineral deposits are often found in sediments.

Stratigraphers examine the order in which rocks have been laid down, their age, and formation.

Volcanologists study volcanoes and volcanic eruptions to help us understand these phenomena and predict when they might happen.

Fossilized rhinoceros skeleton
Chiseling away loose rock

Geophysics

This branch of geoscience involves the application of physical laws and principles to the study of the Earth and the solar system. Scientists explore the Earth's interior through physical measurements collected at the Earth's surface, or from aircraft or satellites.

GEOPHYSICISTS use the principles of physics to study the Earth's interior. They focus on an investigation of its gravitational, electric, and magnetic fields.

EXPLORATION GEOPHYSICISTS use data from seismology magnetic fields, and electrical fields to find oil.

SEISMOLOGISTS study earthquakes and analyze the movement of seismic waves to interpret the structure of the Earth.

SPACE GEOPHYSICISTS are scientists who study life and conditions in the solar system.

A seismologist checks a seismograph

Atmospheric science

The branch of geoscience known as atmospheric science studies the behavior of the Earth's atmosphere and its interaction with the Sun.

ATMOSPHERIC SCIENTISTS study weather processes. They also follow the global dynamics of climate, examine solar radiation and its effects, and make connections between atmospheric chemistry and ozone depletion, climate change, and pollution.

ATMOSPHERIC CHEMISTS study the various chemical processes occurring in the atmosphere; for example, the relationship between the ozone layer and CFCs.

ATMOSPHERIC PHYSICISTS study the effects of various forces on the behavior of the Earth's atmosphere.

CLIMATOLOGISTS look at the bigger picture, studying the average weather conditions and changes in temperature over a period of years.

METEOROLOGISTS study the atmosphere and the movement and energy changes within it—including the weather. Meteorologists use their findings to help predict weather conditions.

A meteorologist observes weather conditions

Space sciences

These scientists explore the realm of space, including everything in the solar system and beyond! You do not have to leave Earth to become a space scientist, but most astronauts who enter NASA's space program have completed extensive studies in the space sciences or related disciplines.

An astrogeologist with a moon rock

ASTRONOMERS study the heavenly bodies, their movements, and location.

ASTROPHYSICISTS examine the physical properties of forces in space, including the dynamics of time and matter.

ASTROGEOLOGISTS study the Moon and other planets to shed new light on the evolution of the solar system.

Oceanography

The study of the Earth's seas is known as oceanography. Oceanography deals with basic scientific study of the oceans and marine life. This science also studies practical problems that affect human life on Earth, such as marine pollution.

OCEANOGRAPHERS investigate all aspects of the undersea world: the physical, chemical, biological, and geological dynamics of the world's oceans.

BIOLOGICAL OCEANOGRAPHERS study life in the ocean, and how it is affected by chemical and physical processes.

CHEMICAL OCEANOGRAPHERS focus on the chemical makeup of the ocean and its relationship to the lithosphere.

Scuba equipment

An oceanographer photographs a fish

Find out more

PLANET EARTH—you've lived here all your life, but there's always more to know about the place we call home. Once you have learned about the incredible forces that make and shape the Earth, exploring the scenic wonders of the great outdoors is even more rewarding. From scorched deserts to lush waterfalls, from soaring mountains to deep canyons, each of Earth's landscapes is a result of a unique geological history. Prefer the great indoors? Check out your local natural history or science museum to uncover more about our amazing planet.

RECORD IN THE ROCKS
Many museum collections display a range of plant and animal fossils, such as this ancient fish fossil. These provide important clues about the age of the rocks in the Earth's crust and the Earth itself.

Cranks turn to move the gears

The globe represents the Earth

AS THE WORLD TURNS
Museum collections may also include some of the instruments Earth scientists use to collect, collate, and display data. This orrery, for example, was used to show the relative size, movement, positions, and orbits of the Earth and other planets in the solar system.

ALL ABOARD
Do you want to experience an oceanographer's job without getting wet? Climb inside a full-sized model of a deep-sea submersible at the Woods Hole Oceanographic Institution in Massachusetts. This craft carries scientists as deep as 12,500 ft (3,810 m) below the ocean waves.

Colorful gems and rocks

EARTH'S TREASURES
A variety of minerals, gems, and rocks of different shapes and colors have been extracted from the Earth. You can see many of these glittering treasures, familiar and unfamiliar, in museum galleries all over the world.

A WALK THROUGH THE EARTH'S PAST

The Earth's history is locked within its rocks, but you don't need to do any digging to explore them. Instead, browse the collections of your local science museum or center. Or visit a museum such as Pittsburgh's Carnegie Museum of Natural History, right. In just a few hours, you will encounter hundreds of amazing specimens that reveal millions of years in the Earth's long history.

A MIGHTY WATERFALL

The best way to appreciate the power of the Earth's forces is to experience it in person. Stand at the base of Yosemite Falls at Yosemite National Park in California, close enough to feel a spray of white mist and hear the water roar and imagine how the pounding water wears away the rocks to shape the land.

LEARNING WITH A TWIST

While firsthand experience is a great way to learn, you don't want to tangle with a tornado. That's why interactive exhibits at many science museums allow you to explore the Earth's forces through simulations, putting a new spin on science education.

THE DAY AFTER TOMORROW?

The Earth's multimillion-year history is the subject of many television documentaries and feature-length movies. Many recent films, such as *The Day After Tomorrow*, raise questions about what may happen in the Earth's future. While these movies are fun, the science behind them can be suspect. Check out the internet to see what the scientific community has to say.

Glossary

ATMOSPHERE The gaseous envelope surrounding the Earth; it consists of oxygen, nitrogen, and other gases.

ATOLL A ring-shaped coral island that nearly or completely surrounds a lagoon.

BASALT A dark, dense volcanic rock commonly found in lava flows.

BATHOLITH A large intrusion of rock (often granite) forming the base of a mountain range.

BLACK SMOKER A chimneylike structure that grows at the spreading ridges on the ocean floor.

BONDING The means by which compounds join together to make molecules.

CONGLOMERATE A rock made up of rock fragments or pebbles cemented together by a substance such as clay or silica.

CONTINENTAL DRIFT The theory dating from the 1960s that the Earth's continents slowly shift their positions as a result of currents in the molten rocks.

CORE The name for the metallic center of the Earth; it has a liquid outer portion and a solid inner part.

CRUST The solid, rocky outer portion or shell of the Earth.

DELTA A deposit of sand and soil (usually triangular) formed at the mouth of a river.

DEPOSITION The process by which layers of sand, clay, minerals, or other building blocks of Earth are set down.

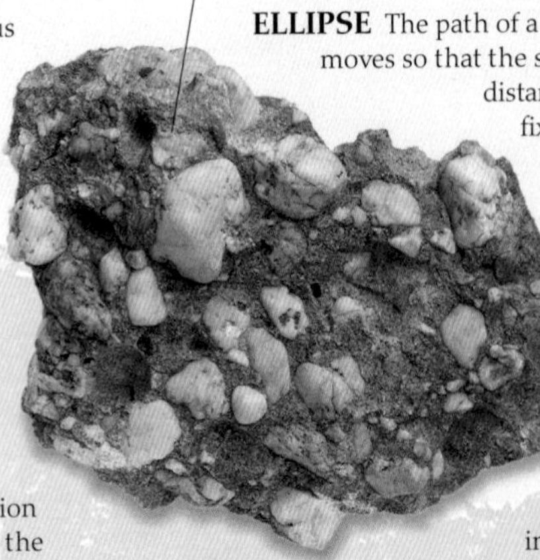
Smaller fragments cemented together by clay or silica
Conglomerate rock

ELLIPSE The path of a point that moves so that the sum of its distances from two fixed points is constant.

EROSION All the ways in which rocks or rock materials are removed and transported to another place, usually under the influence of gravity.

ESTUARY An inlet or arm of the sea, especially a wide mouth of a river where the tide meets the current.

FAULT A fracture or zone of fractures (fault zone) in the Earth's crust resulting from movement.

FENG SHUI The ancient Chinese practice of landscape divining.

FRACTURE A crack or split in the Earth's rocks, or the texture of the broken surface of a mineral.

GABBRO A dark, coarse-grained rock of crystalline texture that forms at spreading centers in rift zones and midocean ridges.

GEOLOGY The science dealing with the physical nature and history of the Earth; it includes the study of the structure and development of the Earth's crust, its composition, and its rocks.

GLACIER A large mass of moving ice and snow found in the high valleys of many mountain ranges.

Deposition shapes coastal beaches like this one

GNEISS A coarse-grained, metamorphic rock that resembles granite.

HORST The name for a raised rock mass between two faults.

HUMUS The organic part of soil; a brown or black substance resulting from the partial decay of plant and animal matter.

IGNEOUS Something produced by volcanic action; for example, the rocks solidified from molten magma at or near the Earth's surface.

ISOSTASY A condition in which there is equal pressure on every side; in geology, this is the equilibrium in large, equal areas of the Earth's crust that is preserved by the force of gravity.

Fiery lava is ejected from a volcano cone

LAVA Molten rock that comes from a volcano; the same rock when cooled at the Earth's surface.

LITHOSPHERE Another name for the crust, which is the solid, rocky part of the Earth.

MAGMA Liquid or molten rock deep within the Earth.

MAGNETIC FIELD A region of space in which there is a measurable amount of magnetic force.

MAGNETOMETER An instrument for measuring magnetic forces.

MANTLE The layer of the Earth's interior between the crust and the core.

METAMORPHIC Of, causing, or formed by a change in form, shape, or structure.

MIDOCEAN RIDGE A long, narrow elevation of land on the seafloor.

MOHS SCALE The scale used to indicate the relative hardness of minerals.

MORAINE The mass of rocks, gravel, sand, and clay carried by a glacier and deposited along its side or lower end.

OCEANOGRAPHY The study of the total environment of Earth's oceans, including the waters, depths, seabeds, marine animals, and plants.

OROGENY The name for the formation of the Earth's mountains through structural disturbances in the crust, especially folding and faulting.

OZONE LAYER The protective layer of the stratosphere that filters the Sun's rays.

PANGAEA The name of the single landmass that split apart about 200 million years ago to form the present-day continents on Earth.

PETROLOGY The study of the classification, location, composition, structure, and origin of rocks.

PHOTOSYNTHESIS The process by which green plants transform radiant energy from the Sun into a chemical form.

PLATE BOUNDARIES Margins that divide up the surface of the Earth.

PLATE TECTONICS The theory that the world is divided into moving plates. New plate material is made all the time at spreading ridges and old plate material is recycled at subduction zones.

PLATEAU A tablelike, elevated area of more or less level land.

PRIMARY WAVES Earthquake waves that travel fastest and are the first to be recorded by a seismograph.

RADIOMETRIC DATING A method of determining the age of rocks from the decay of their radioactive elements. This method has provided the strongest evidence of the age of even the oldest of the Earth's rocks.

RADIUS A straight line extending from the center to the periphery of a sphere.

RIFT A large fault along which movement is mostly lateral, creating a rift valley.

ROCK CYCLE The continuous action of renewal of the Earth's surface: igneous rocks come into contact with the atmosphere and change; these rocks are eroded to form sediments; and sediments become sedimentary rock and can be changed into metamorphic rock or heated to make new igneous rock.

SALINITY The measurement of the concentration of salt in water.

SEDIMENT Matter that is deposited by water or wind. Sedimentary rock is formed by the deposit of sediments.

SEISMIC WAVES The name for waves from an earthquake that travel outward in all directions and can be refracted back to the Earth's surface.

SEISMOGRAPH A sensitive device that measures an earthquake's waves; a seismometer records the movement of the ground near a quake.

SHEAR WAVE A seismic wave that shears the rocks it passes through; shear waves cannot travel through liquids.

SILICATE A combination of the elements silicon and oxygen that makes up 75 percent of the Earth's rocks.

SOIL CREEP A constant downhill movement of soil under the influence of gravity.

SOLAR WIND Streams of ionized gas particles emitted by the Sun in all directions; solar winds can reach speeds of up to 2 million mph (3.2 million kph).

Striae were left by rocks carried in a passing glacier

Striae (scratches) on rock

STRATOSPHERE The atmospheric zone above the troposphere containing the Earth's ozone layer.

STRIAE Scratches left on the surface of rock when a glacier passes over it.

SUBDUCTION ZONE An area where the ocean floor subducts into the mantle. The sinking basaltic rock is melted, and this new magma eventually makes its way back to the Earth's surface.

TECTONICS See Plate tectonics.

THERMOSPHERE The name for the part of the Earth's atmosphere that is farthest from its surface.

THRUST FAULT A fracture in the Earth along which movement has occurred; it is often formed where tectonic plates collide.

THRUST SHEET The upper section of rocks that is pushed in thrust faulting.

TOPOGRAPHY The surface features of the Earth, or the representation of these features on a map or in a drawing.

Stalactites hang from a cave roof

TOR A high, rocky hill or crag.

TROPOSPHERE The layer of the Earth's atmosphere that is closest to land; weather is confined to this layer.

UPLIFT In geology, the vertical movement of large sections of crust.

VESICLE A small, round cavity in volcanic rock produced by air or gas bubbles in the molten rock.

STALACTITE An icicle-shaped deposit of carbonate of lime hanging from the roof of a cave.

STALAGMITE A cone-shaped deposit of carbonate of lime built up on a cave floor from something, such as a stalactite, dripping from above.

STRATIGRAPHY The arrangement of rocks in layers, or strata.

VOLCANO A vent in the Earth's crust through which molten rock, ash, gas, and rock fragments are ejected from the interior.

WAVELETS The name for small ripples in a body of water.

WEATHERING The physical and chemical effects of the forces of weather on rock surfaces.

Index

Acknowledgments

The publisher would like to thank: Henry Buckley, Andrew Clarke, Alan Hart, and Chris Jones at the Natural History Museum; Professor Ken McClay, Sun Professor of Structural Geology at Royal Holloway University of London; John Catt at Rothamsted Experimental Station; the staff at the Institute of Oceanographic Sciences Deacon Laboratories; the staff at the British Antarctic Survey; Brian Taylor and Fergus McTaggart at the British Geological Survey; Frances Halpin for assistance with the chemistry experiments; The Old Southern Forge for the iron on page 29. **Illustrations:** Stephen Bull **Photography:** Andy Crawford, Mike Dunning, Neil Fletcher, Steve Gorton, Colin Keates, Dave King, James Stephenson, Harry Taylor, Peter York **Index:** Helen Peters. **Proofreading:** Monica Byles

Picture credits
t=top b=bottom c=center l=left r=right a=above

Alamy Images: whyeyephotography.com 30clb. B & C Alexander 58b. Biofotos/Heather Angel 17tl. Bodleian Library, Oxford 9br; 9tr. Bridgeman/ Royal Geographical Society 8tl; /Louvre, Paris 52tl. Oriental Section, Bristol Museums and Art Gallery 9b. British Antarctic Society 6br; 19tr; 32bl; / E.Wolff 19br; /R.Mulvaney 19bc; /NOAA 39br. British Geological Survey 7clb; 21br; 61tl. Bruce Coleman Picture Library /Jules Cowan 17clb; /M.P.L.Fogden 20 cl. Corbis: Wesley Cheek / AFLO / Nippon News 42tl, Chris Harris / All Canada Photos 58cl, Momatiuk - Eastcott 58bl. Dreamstime.com: Manfred Harzl 40cra, Mrpeak 63cr, Pedroramos 13bl. Getty Images: Apic / Hulton Archive 30tl, Fairfax Media 42cr. James Davis Photography 50-51b. Joe Cornish 55l. John Catt 52r; 52bc. Mary Evans Picture Library 22cr; 24tl; 30bc; 34 cr; 40tl; 60tl; /Explorer Biblioteca Reale, Torino 8bl. ffotograff/Charles Aithie 50cl; 52bl; 56tr; /Jill Ranford 51tc. Greenpeace/Loor 18bl. Gwynedd Archive Service 28cb. Robert Harding Picture Library 37tr; 37bl; 39cla; 44clb; 47cr; 63tr; /Y. Arthus Bertrand Explorer 56cr; / Margaret Collier 56cl; /Ian Griffiths 50tr. Hulton Deutsch 31 tl. Image Bank/Joanna MacCarthy 41cr; /H.Wendler 53tr. Institute of Oceanographic Sciences: Deacon Laboratory 38tr; /MIAS 33tr. Impact/Martin Black 9bl. Mansell Collection 8cr; 8br; 18tl; 34tr; 46tl; 60tr; 62tr. NASA 6tl; 10tl; 11tr; 11tc; 12bc; 34br; 49tl; 49c; 57tl. National Archives of Canada 41 tr; 62cib. National Maritime Museum Publications 30br. National Oceanic and Atmospheric Administration/ National Geophysical Data Center 36bl; 36tl; 37c; 37tcl; 37br. Natural History Museum Picture Library 13cbr. Image Select/Ann Ronan 22tl. Clive Oppenheimer 25l. Oxford Scientific Films/John Downer 49tr; /Mills Tandy 55br; /Konrad Wothe 46cr. Planet Earth Picture Agency/Peter Atkinson 10cr; /Peter David 32tl; Ivor Edmonds 59tr;/David George 24c. Princeton University: Department of Geological and Geophysical Sciences 38tl. Science Photo Library/Dr Gene Feldman/NASA GSFC 32c; /Mark Bond 26tl; /Tony Craddock 48c; /John Downer 37bc; /European Space Agency 1c; / Douglas Faulkner 38cl; /James King-Holmes 61cr; 61crb;/G. Muller, Struers MBH 29tc; /NASA 37tl; 45cla, 58cra; /Peter Ryan Scripps 38cr; /Soames Summerhays 45b; /U.S. Geological Survey 37tcr; 43cra; /Tom Van Sant/Geosphere Project, Santa Monica 14tr; 18cl; 18c. Scripps Institute of Oceanography 32cr. Simon Petroleum 40bc. Frank Spooner Picture Library/Giboux Liais. 43cl; / Planchenault Front Cover. Clive Streeter 46clb; 54clb; 54br; 55tr; 59tc; 63c. U.S. Geological Survey 48tr. Susanna van Rose 29bl; 60clb. Vienna University-Institute of Geology 42crb. Alfred-Wegener Institute: Andreas Frenzel 35tr. Carnegie Museum of Natural History: 69tc Corbis: Annie Griffiths Belt 66b; Jonathan Blair 66tr; Ralph A. Clevenger 64bl; Stephen Frink 67br; Wolfgang Kaehler 64tr; Will & Deni McIntyre 64br; Jim Reed 67cr; Roger Ressmeyer 67bl; Vince Streano 67tr; Courtesy of Twentieth Century Fox/ Bureau L.A.Collections 69br
DK: 54tl; Rough Guides 68-69, 70 tl; Satellite Imagemap Copyright / 1996-2003 Planetary Visions 6bl; Tina Chambers, Courtesy of the National Maritime Museum, London 69tr; Frank Greenaway 65tr; John Heseltine 68tl: Colin Keates, Courtesy of the Natural History Museum, London 7bl, 68bl, 68br, 71tr; Rob Reichenfeld 70bl; Kim Sayer 68c; Harry Taylor 65cl; Francesca Yorke 71bl Photo Researchers, Inc.: Samuel Ashfield 68-69c; B. Edmaier 70cr
University of Colorado Courtesy of NOAA: 64tl Woods Hole Oceanographic Institution: Shelley Dawicki 68bl

Jacket images: *Front:* Dorling Kindersley: NASA c, Natural History Museum, London tl, tc; *Back:* Dorling Kindersley: Edward Laurence Associates - modelmaker c, Natural History Museum, London tl, br

Wallchart credits: Alamy Images: Gabbro crb; Corbis: Daisy Gilardini / Science Faction fcrb, Jim Wark / Visuals Unlimited cr; Dorling Kindersley: Satellite Imagemap Copyright / 1996-2003 Planetary Visions c, Natural History Museum, London tr, tr/ (gold crystals), cb, cb/ (Magnifying Lens), cb/ (Chisel), cb/ (Sharp Chisel), cb/ (obsidian), cb/ (Conglomerate Rock), The Science Museum, London clb; Dreamstime.com: Marcello Mantia br; Getty Images: Dea Picture Library tl; NASA: Johnson Space Center cl; Courtesy of the National Science Foundation: Peter Rejcek bl

With the exception of the items listed above, and the objects from the Science Museum, London on pages 17cr, 12cl, 20tr, and those from the Oxford University Museum on pages 12rc and 62cl, the objects on pages 3tr, 4tr, 4tlc, 4b, 6tl, 14l, 15, 18/19c, 17bc, 17tr, 17tl, 24b, 27tl, 27r, 29l, 33b, 41l, 41b, 43b, 46l, 46c, 46b, 48/49b, 53tl, 53b, 57tr, 57c, 56/57b, 59bl, 59bl, 61tr are all in the collections of the Natural History Museum, London.

All other images © Dorling Kindersley.
For further information see:
www.dkimages.com

Harris County Public Library
Houston, Texas